PRAISE FOR *GETTING IN BY STANDING OUT*

"I love this book! *Getting IN by Standing OUT* is a straight-talking, strategic book—a business plan for getting into college that informs students and parents about the competitive college admissions process and how to stand out in the crowd. It is an aspirational work, with personal stories of students across all talents, majors, and backgrounds—teaching all students how to allow their REAL selves to shine, unlock their gifts, become *extrapreneurial* leaders, and present their authentic talents and skills to get ACCEPTED. The overarching message of the book is that young people should see high school as the start to an adventure of finding their authentic selves…not just for college but for life. 'They won't believe what they can do!'"

Maxine Clark, founder of
Build-A-Bear Workshop and *Education Community Citizen*

"Are you worried about what other families of high achieving children know that you don't about getting your child into a great college? A best-fit college? An intellectually challenging college?

Dr. Bedor has written the seminal field manual for the new reality of college admissions. I couldn't put this book down. There is strategic counsel for achieving success all the way through the rigorous high school curriculum gauntlet. There are out-of-the-box ideas for meaningful impact and engagement that current Admissions demands. There's step-by-step inspiration for creating powerful and authentic personal statements and essays; and student stories of leadership, struggle, and success you won't want to miss. It's a must read for every high school student, parent, and guidance counselor.

Parents: you only have ONE chance to get this right. Don't blow it."

Richard Rossi, founder of
The Congress of Future Medical Leaders and
The Congress of Future Science and Technology Leaders

"Dr. Deborah Bedor's *Getting* **IN** *by Standing* **OUT**: *The New Rules for Admission to America's Best Colleges* is an essential resource for college-bound students and their parents. Dr. Bedor provides practical and entertaining advice for young scholars of all interests, from entrepreneurs, scientists, musicians, and athletes to those still seeking to discover their true passions. As a strong believer in the power of youth, I am delighted that this guide is available to our young people to help them access the education and experience they need to fulfill their dreams."

Claes Nobel, chair of
The National Society of High School Scholars and
senior member of the *Nobel Family*

"*Getting* **IN** *by Standing* **OUT** is a 'must-have' for any parent or high school student in the midst of the college application madness. Whether the process is daunting and seemingly overwhelming, or you simply want the most valuable insights to finding an advantage in the world of admissions, Dr. Bedor's book is a fascinating and inspiring read. Having written a play about the expectations of the world of private kindergarten admissions in NYC, I particularly admire Dr. Bedor's ability to comment intelligently on the heightened level of stress that parents and students face, while simultaneously offering unique and creative steps for effective college preparation. Many students spend months or even years pretending to be something they are not for the purpose of "looking good" on an application, but *Getting* **IN** *by Standing* **OUT** shows these students how to uncover authentic and creative ways to excel and make an impact during their formative high school years. The tools provided in this book can help students and their parents rise to the challenge of application season – and their college days ahead – with their best foot forward."

Andy Sandberg, *Tony Award-winning* producer
of the Broadway revival of *HAIR*; author and director of
APPLICATION PENDING –
A Comedy about Kindergarten Admissions

"This is the treasure map you've been looking for. The preeminent guide for students applying to top tier and Ivy League schools, *Getting* **IN** *by Standing* **OUT** is also, hands down, the best available guide for any student seeking to be admitted to the nation's top arts schools and music conservatories. The young fine and performing arts talents of the world need a champion and counselor, and Dr. Bedor's extensive background in the arts, plus her sage and sound academic and leadership advice will squarely place your talent in the best possible light for acceptance, and present you as a whole person to the finest schools in the world. With this brilliant book in hand, take courage!"

Christopher Mangum, *New York State Teacher of the Year*
finalist and *Emmy Award-winning* composer

Getting IN by Standing OUT

Getting IN *by* *Standing* OUT

*The New Rules for Admission
to America's Best Colleges*

DR. DEBORAH BEDOR

Published by Advantage, Charleston, South Carolina.
Member of Advantage Media Group.

ADVANTAGE is a registered trademark and the Advantage colophon is a trademark of Advantage Media Group, Inc.

Printed in the United States of America.

ISBN: 978-1-59932-559-0   6 0973517
LCCN: 2015936963   8/16

This publication is designed to provide accurate and authoritative information in regard to the subject matter covered. It is sold with the understanding that the publisher is not engaged in rendering legal, accounting, or other professional services. If legal advice or other expert assistance is required, the services of a competent professional person should be sought.

Advantage Media Group is proud to be a part of the Tree Neutral® program. Tree Neutral offsets the number of trees consumed in the production and printing of this book by taking proactive steps such as planting trees in direct proportion to the number of trees used to print books. To learn more about Tree Neutral, please visit **www.treeneutral.com**. To learn more about Advantage's commitment to being a responsible steward of the environment, please visit **www.advantagefamily.com/green**

Advantage Media Group is a publisher of business, self-improvement, and professional development books and online learning. We help entrepreneurs, business leaders, and professionals share their Stories, Passion, and Knowledge to help others Learn & Grow. Do you have a manuscript or book idea that you would like us to consider for publishing? Please visit **advantagefamily.com** or call **1.866.775.1696**.

To the precious memory of my mother and father,
Shirley and George Bedor.
You were my inspiration in all things and still are.

TABLE OF CONTENTS

INTRODUCTION

Let me be something every minute of every hour of my life.
—Betty Smith, A Tree Grows in Brooklyn

A bright-eyed, well-groomed young man of 17 entered my studio with his mother. The boy was empty-handed—but his mom carried a folder packed to capacity. That was my first clue.

After preliminary greetings, we sat, and I began to take the boy's vitals. His name: Matt; his GPA: 4.5; his standardized test scores: 780, 800, 760; his brave new world of choice: computer science.

"What a great start, Matt!" I began. "And what do you enjoy outside of school?"

"Oh, he works at Computer Associates twice a week after school," answered Mom.

"Dr. B asked what I enjoy, not where I work," Matt protested softly.

"*And* he plays cello with the regional youth orchestra," she continued. "First chair!"

"Maaaaa…" whined Matt.

"And he's building an app to help local animal shelters showcase 'the pet of the week' for adoption. We thought that would look good when we apply to Cornell."

"Look, Mom, that doesn't answer the question. The question is about what I enjoy outside of class, and what I enjoy is technical climbing. But there's no team for that, no varsity letter, so we agreed I couldn't use it for a college essay. Besides, it's not intellectual enough to get me in anyway."

In moments, this smart, confident young man had been reduced to a bundle of nerves and insecurity. This is what a gross miscommunication of the college application process has been doing to our best and brightest. They hear it from their guidance counselors, from devoted parents, from their friends and friends' parents, and even from their colleges of choice: "To get into this *college* you must be interesting in the *right fields* and show a thread of passion and intellect all through high school."

No, my friend: To get into this *life* you must be interesting and build a thread of passion in the field of *your* choice. Our lives are judged on two things—impact and engagement. How have we impacted our families, our professions, and our communities by pushing boundaries or advocating for what we believe? How have we engaged with the people, the ideas, the causes, and our own intellects to move life's needle in new, positive ways? We can all identify people of passion and action. A certain level of sophistication can be found in their speech, their writing, and their considerations. They have made themselves fascinating. The process is no different for high school students and their college applications. Please understand that colleges care very much about your authentic journey through high school because that journey will uncover your passions, your impact, and your engagement. Admissions will ask: how have you invested in yourself that makes you interesting enough for them to invest in you? The search for your authentic self in high school *reveals* the character and intellectual vitality that Admissions needs to understand in order to *accept* you.

So if you're a rock climber, do it with gusto. Tell us about your first time bouldering—the pounding excitement on the approach and how you learned fearlessness after the lunge. Then tell us how climbing has helped you in life. If your heart is on the stage, don't worry that actors from your high school have not typically been accepted to your college of choice. Go ahead and follow your artistic passion. Take on as many roles as you can. Tell us why you do it: What gift does it give you? How does acting make you wiser and more worldly? If you're passionate about your calling, Admissions will be excited about you.

If you're a storyteller, go have experiences so you can tell better stories. Travel, talk to strangers. Open up to us about what you've learned. If you're a chef (with awesome grades and scores), please don't be afraid that Yale won't think it's intellectual enough or Duke won't think you're cool enough or Stanford won't think you're "techie" enough. Instead, rejoice in telling us how flavors heighten your sensory perceptions, why you love exploration into ethnic dishes, and how that has broadened your perspective. Cook for a cause at a high school charitable event; draw up a business plan for a new food venue that donates profits to good causes. Again, if you're excited about your skill, we will be too!

So when you hear the noise coming from administrators, counselors, and loved ones about how you need good grades and scores, plus some sort of developed passion to get accepted to college, I want you to automatically substitute the word life for college and see how much more empowered that makes you feel; how much more authentic your reasons for achieving become when you're doing it to find out who you are; how many more chances you're willing to take to fail and start again, and build, and succeed.

This time is all about you. Begin the journey of finding your authentic selves. T.E. Lawrence said: "All men dream, but not equally. Those who dream in the dark recesses of the night awake in the day to find all was vanity. But the dreamers of day are dangerous men [human beings], for they may act their dreams with open eyes, and make it possible."

The ambition to build yourself, to push and motivate yourself, and take yourself to a new place is the stuff of a successful path through life, not just a successful path to college. That'll happen too, but it should be a by-product of finding out just how much you've got to give during your young, scrappy years. Past success predicts future success. If you find out during high school that you can succeed in something—anything—you will carry that memory and that success to the campus and beyond, through your professional life.

You're probably wondering what became of Matt. He did wind up writing his essay about years of passion for technical climbing; and his breadth of knowledge about the field together with the tough, focused grit and natural leadership and decision-making skills he demonstrated through that essay brought him an acceptance to his top Ivy League choice.

You see, when all else is equal (good grades, recommendations, test scores), it is the glimmer of your authentic voice, and how you've built on your passions, that will get you accepted. You don't have to know who you are for life...just find out who you are for now. Don't let a misguided system make you feel otherwise.

This book is here to help you cut your way through the underbrush—the bad if well-intended advice and the temptation to make yourself over into what you think your dream schools are looking for—to the path that will bring you home to *you*. There is no right combination of things that gets a student accepted to a top college. There is only the right student for that college; and we find you by reading your authentic journey.

CHAPTER ONE

WHY MOST OF WHAT YOU KNOW ABOUT COLLEGE ADMISSIONS IS WRONG

Today you are You, that is truer than true.
There is no one alive who is Youer than You.
—Dr. Seuss

Well, the rules have changed—again. It used to be that having excellent grades and high scores would get you accepted to your school of choice. Then, you had to be the Renaissance guy or gal—a calculus and computer science whiz who built apps, also got As in AP English Literature, placed at the International Science and Engineering Fair (ISEF), and won the class president runoff. Today, the idea of a deeply developed passion in some intellectual or leadership space is what's intoxicatingly appealing to Admissions.

In my 25 years as a college admissions specialist, I've seen it all. I've worked with celebrity clients who had already found their life's work but needed help finding the right fit for college; students with tremendous academic gifts but no leadership skills; students with leadership skills but few academic gifts; students with lopsided but marvelous intellect and special talent; performance and fine artists who spent high school in conservatories but didn't want to continue in a professional arts environment for the next four years; athletes who were nationally ranked and recruited and others who just wanted to play for enjoyment; valedictorians who were paralyzed with fear of applying to the Ivies and not getting in after sacrificing their high school years to their studies; solid B students who had not yet found their passion or direction; struggling students who thought a four-year college was out of the question; and students with quirks or special needs that needed to be welcomed and addressed. And this is just a sample of the many wonderful, spirited, kind, and exceptional young people I've had the pleasure of mentoring and molding for college. They all had one thing in common—all of these kids were totally convinced that everything special and fascinating they accomplished during high school was for the sole purpose of getting them into college and had nothing to do with opening doors for them in life.

Here's the thing: *Your well-meaning and overworked guidance counselor, your friends, your dear parents—all of these people who are telling you what you have to do to get into college—are wrong.*

You've heard the mantra since middle school: You have to be a loyal and talented athlete in your favorite sport, you have to play an instrument, you have to decide if you're going to med school by freshman year of high school so that you can take all the right AP courses and get the right internship at the right lab or medical center, you have to audition with your instrument by 7th grade so that you can be in a weekend conservatory by 8th grade (even if all you possess is technical facility and unusual patience for Hanon exercises). If you don't have musical, dance, or dramatic talent, you should at least be creating apps. Don't know what you want to do? Start a business! Like to argue? Shoot for law. Good in STEM? That's it! Engineering school for you—(hope you love calculus, differential equations, and have a warm spot for C, C++, Java, and Python). Everyone who has an interest in your future has hammered in that these are the things that will tilt the admission decision in your favor—regardless of whether or not you have a passion to follow them.

But it's *just not true.*

NURTURING YOUR "EXCEPTIONAL TILT"

Instead, you have to have what I call "exceptional tilt"; a commitment to a personal quest, passion, or cause that's in line with your gifts, your strengths, and *your* ambitions (not someone else's version of your ambitions). This tilt isn't just something you put on, like a coat, to impress Admissions but an important piece of your journey of self-discovery, one that will serve you throughout your life. The adventure and challenges in finding and nurturing that tilt give you a story worth telling and one that your college of choice will be interested to hear. For sure, a couple of your exceptional qualities and the right focused project taken together would certainly make a lovely college application package, but finding that rewarding and advantageous combination for each individual is an art, not a checklist to fill out. Knowing the things you're good at doesn't make your journey a done deal, and the fact that you haven't explored a talent doesn't mean it is out of the question. Find the thing that fascinates you, and you will become fascinating. Your application will speak with a sophistication of thought and tone that we don't often see in applications of students who just follow the "right" activity path.

In high school, you're in the process of learning what your authentic self is. The extended process of self-exploration that we call "college" is there so that you can begin to climb out of childhood and step up to your talents, intellect, and leadership level. Everything you do in high school in an effort to improve yourselves for college is, in fact, improving you for *life*.

What does this mean to you, high school student and college hopeful? It's a fast-paced world, and you're coming up in it, so by high school your individual exploration and creativity need to be pretty fast-paced too. Remember, it's what you do beyond the walls of high school that makes the difference in your college application and prepares you for an interesting life. And you'll find a much easier trip if you travel this road as yourself.

That said, you still have to be on top of your grades and your test scores—that hasn't changed. Suppose you're an activist out to change the world, and you've started your own public service organization or charity. This is terrific, as long as changing the world doesn't change your grades. Many young activists get so involved with their speaking and traveling calendars that they forget about their testing calendars. It's a simple rule: if your grades will suffer or your focused study for tests will be interrupted, then don't accept that public appearance.

A hard fact: you're never so special that colleges don't think they can create the same great class without you. Never give a college a reason to reject you—be smart about balancing your talents, competitions, and engagements with your academic realities. If admissions officers think that your application and résumé demonstrate more emphasis on creating celebrity for yourself than on love of learning and classroom zeal, all that travel and those absences from class will add up to the impression that academics come last in your life. The process of engaging in scholarship is part of discovering and building your authentic self. If your GPA and standardized scores stay within the mid-high range of your schools of choice, then you're doing things right.

People always ask me, "Will a 4.0 and 2400 get me into the Ivy League school of my dreams?" And I always say, "Well, it won't keep you *out*."

The problem is, there are thousands of students with those numbers—as hard as that is to believe. Some come by them naturally, others through very hard work, and still others through daily tutoring. Regardless of how they get there, they get there. The transcript will look the same for all of them. The only things that will make the best stand out from the rest are their teachers' recommendations (although nearly everyone in this category will most likely have glowing recommendations) and their uncommon, authentic, individual edge.

The truth in today's admissions market is that, if you're aiming for a top-tier or Ivy League school, and you have SAT scores at or above 730 or ACTs at or above 34 and a GPA around 95 unweighted in an all or almost all-AP schedule, **you have the same shot as does a 4.0 valedictorian *if* you have more interesting or compelling leadership, talents, or extra-curricular involvement *outside* of your school and/or on a national basis.** Additionally, if you have won any national awards for that talent or leadership, it puts you in a category above. Rejoice!

Are you a leader? And by "leader," I don't mean having run for student office and won; a lot of students have done that. I mean, have you been fascinated enough by something to have stepped out of your high school to make an impact on the lives of others? Have you started a business, organization, or project to provide for the community at home or abroad? Do you have a social or political platform about which you speak at schools, conferences, or TEDx? Are you a passionate science researcher? Have you written a novel or play or created a blog or website that has become popular? Are you a belly dancer or an award-winning ballroom dancer? Do you build apps that matter? If so, how many users do you have, and whom do those apps help? Have you led instead of joined? Top colleges are not interested in members; they are interested in leaders.

Maybe your special tilt is to the arts. Are you taking the initiative to nurture that talent? Do you attend a weekend conservatory program in music, art, dance, or theater? Do you have a portfolio or video reel to show? Have you worked in an arts field after school, and if so, what have you gained from this that can't be gained in a classroom? Write about it in your college application.

Can you show, through your high school career, in some way, that you have the gusto, intellect, and curiosity to grab opportunities whenever and wherever they are presented to you? If so, your college choices will see that you're the type of student who will make the most out of your college career. Any way you can show this gusto will throw points in your direction.

Remember that admissions is a holistic process at the top schools and throughout many schools in our nation. Nobody looks for a straight-A student with no personality, gumption, or leadership. Nobody wants someone who is a member of every club but who has probably spent the last three and a half years studying in a room seven days a week. If you are an excellent student and develop outside passions that leap off the page and find a creative and illustrative way in which to present them, you will be able to compete with any valedictorian.

DEFINING LEADERSHIP

When you hear "leadership," does it sound like something you could never do? Leadership is often viewed as one person's ability to command the support, efforts, and work of a group toward a specific goal. However, no one ever said leadership only referred to being the president of a school club, the founder of an organization, or the political force behind a new movement. Leadership is a state of being. Leadership means aspiring to be inspirational. It means moving on what you are passionate about or interested in to make something positive happen. Every person has the ability to create some positive change somewhere. The trick to becoming a leader is figuring out what specific cause or purpose fascinates you.

A note about leadership: it's not enough to merely hold a position of leadership. You must *take* your idea or followers or project somewhere. This same definition applies to how you demonstrate leadership to admissions officers. Don't just write a title on your résumé. Explain to Admissions how you brought further success to the group, project, or club you lead. What they are looking for is regional, national, or international success; raising funds; or helping to create something of value in your school, town, or city through the group under your leadership. The best of all is out-of-school leadership that shows you followed your heart and founded an organization or social enterprise or became the leader of an advocacy group, for instance, for education or the environment. The most impressive validation of your work would ideally come from having won some recognition for your organization or business or perhaps being invited to present at a TEDx event.

Admissions officers will ask the question:
Where is the thread of passion?

- Have you been consistently involved in the success and/or leadership of one or two particular clubs, organizations, or business ventures? What elements demonstrate that long-term interest? Awards? Grants from companies or social organizations recognizing your work and funding a particular project you are creating? Attending summer programs that will improve your knowledge base, leadership skills, field or research skills?

- Have you engaged in high school club hopping (which has nothing to do with DJs and dance)—what I call *activity bombing*? Does it look like you engaged in résumé padding? Or is there long-term commitment to one or two projects/clubs?

- Word to the wise: Be sure to begin your involvement in these one or two organizations, clubs, or businesses as early in high school as possible (of course, freshman year would be awesome). If you don't, then Admissions can't see a thread of passion or leadership skill over a long period of time. It's not the title that you finally receive junior year as officer of a school club that will get you noticed–it's the individual motivation and successful effort you've been putting into the leadership game since freshman or sophomore year. Those are the students who have stories to tell: the ones who can write about taking an idea through brainstorming, failures, and successes. Those are the kind of passionate can-do students that admissions officers want on campus. Remember–the best guarantee of future success is past success.

- And…at least three days a week, get out of your school building after the bell rings and make something happen in your community! Opportunities are everywhere.

In chapters to come, we'll discuss the ways that you can use the opportunities beyond the walls of your high school to create your meaningful, authentic journey—a journey that will set you apart not only in your future career but also to the gatekeepers in Admissions. You have the potential to be so much more than any admissions officer could ever imagine. WATCH!

CHAPTER TWO

INSIDE THE ADMISSIONS OFFICE

Students (and their parents) put a lot of effort into trying to second-guess what goes through the minds of the admissions office staff who will ultimately read and judge their applications. Who are these people who seem to have so much power over your future? What are they really looking for, and what's the best way to get past these gatekeepers and into the school of your choosing?

Admissions officers today are different than those who held these jobs in the past. Many hold bachelor's degrees from the school you want to attend. Many hold master's degrees. Many are newly graduated and are looking for a way up into university administration or see their jobs as a way station between careers. These are very savvy readers. These are readers who care a great deal about the students they go to bat for, as well as about creating an exceptional class. They will be risk averse if they see grades or scores that don't match up with the rigors of their institution's academics. Of course, admissions officers have to ask the mundane questions: Will this great candidate be likely to accept our admission offer? Do we already have representative students from this rural zip code? Has a university faculty member sent a letter of recommendation on an applicant's behalf? You get the idea. However true to life those questions are in top admissions offices around the country, little is more important than the value they believe you might bring to their campus.

As they say in the TV talk show business, admissions officers want the *"get"* that is going to change the shape of a campus, a department, a classroom, or a dorm. Your scores should be in the top 25 percent of what they normally admit, but beyond that, it's all about the special quality, achievement, or name you've made for yourself during your journey of self-discovery that you can now share with the school of your dreams. Admissions officers will invest "capital" in you if they see that *both* your academics and your interests outside of school add up to a successful and interesting future college student. If you've taken the time to begin considering who you are, what is meaningful to you, and how you might make a mark in the world, you are already ahead of so many students in the applicant pool. In fact, even if you have run with an idea—a business, an app, a service platform—and failed (an experience that could turn into an explorative and inspirational personal statement, depending on how you express what you've learned from that failure), you will still find yourself with many more top college acceptances than your peers. When my students begin finding their authentic and interesting selves by junior year, they gain *acceptance* at an extraordinary rate.

ADMISSIONS OFFICERS AS INVESTORS

Why do I use the word "investor"? Well, think about it; we say things like: "This is how I spent my life" or we ask: "How did you spend your summer? How did you spend your college years?" Note the use of the word "spend"? Clearly, the underlying message is that each of these represents an investment of capital in a significant experience in your existence on this planet. So why would it seem odd or calculating that college admissions officers would look at each student as an investment and see themselves as strategic investors? They spend their admissions cycle deciding whether you're a good investment for the school—someone they believe will help make their school more interesting, lively, and creative, and someone for whom the school can provide the most meaningful platform or diving board to future success. Their job, after all, is to protect the school's brand—because at a top-tier school, that brand is a very valuable commodity. The student most likely to be admitted is the one whom the admissions officer sees as most likely to bring value to that brand. What kind of return on investment are *you* going to give them?

Success leaves tracks. If you can show that you're invested in your interests and can juggle leadership, talents, and a rigorous course load in high school, chances are you're going to be a good investment for college.

NO STUNTS, PLEASE

If you need a laugh, try googling "crazy college admission stories"—then imagine how tired your admissions officers must be of the parade of stunts they see from hopeful admits.

Don't be that guy/gal whose crazy stunt goes viral—but still doesn't get admitted. Be the person they can't say no to, not the one they can't wait to say no to.

Smart kids often do dumb things when they try to "game" the admissions office—stuff like padding their résumés, overstating their accomplishments, or overloading their essays with what they think will appeal to Admissions' sympathies. We'll cover such things in detail in later chapters, but understand from the outset that these folks have seen it all and aren't easily snowed, so it's best not to try. Honesty is always the best policy. However, that doesn't mean that you should write an artless college essay—just pouring stats and experiences onto the page. You must bring some craftsmanship to the effort of presenting your best, true self to these savvy gatekeepers and make it as easy as possible for them to say Yes.

Be careful with how you describe your activities, such as the number of hours spent (admissions officers know there are only 24 hours in a day and you can't be volunteering or playing your cello for all of them), work that you've done, and organizations you've run. Also, be judicious in how many recommendations you request and from whom. Lots of students try to pull the wool over the eyes of what they *think* are unsuspecting admissions officers, but you really don't want to find out what happens when you misrepresent! If you have worked hard and excelled, your résumé and application will tell the story without needing to call in ten recommendations from friends of friends on the board of trustees of your desired university and without having to double the number of hours you enter on the Common App for each of your activities.

If there were dips on your transcript—issues during school that affected your grades in a serious way—write about them in full and send that to Admissions via email as well as in hard copy via snail mail. Your admissions officer will want to know if there were concrete reasons for grades dropping from an A to a C, or for a disciplinary action. Perhaps there was illness or a death in the family, or a parent out of work; maybe your health was suffering or you had a trauma or other stressor. All these things should be explained, not only by you but by your guidance counselor as well. But please note—do not call attention to that one semester in which you dropped from an A to a B in calculus. It's a tough course. Everybody knows that, and it's likely that an admission committee will not even think twice about that drop if all of your other grades remain excellent. Don't make a problem where none exists.

When admissions officers see a detailed and well thought out application that presents a uniquely intellectual or cleverly humorous voice, and a long thread of service or developed talent, they are more likely to move that student to the next round of committees. Do remember that your grades and scores have to be in the ballpark for each college, because admissions officers *are* taking a risk by putting their name on a vote for your acceptance. They lose credibility professionally if you, the student they believed in, can't cut the work on campus when you get there in the fall. So prepare your high school life with thought, hard work, and creativity, knowing that Admissions will also work very hard to bring in students who are the best investments for that university.

A hint: When you write your applications, do extol the virtues of liberal arts if you're a humanities or social science person. Professors in those fields don't like that they're being assigned second place after STEM in high school curricula. After all, liberal arts students are the embodiment of respect for the written word, empathy, and broad, global understanding. Through their studies, they have looked through literary, artistic, psychological, and historical windows into human behavior, deep-seated emotions, and predilections. Truthfully, without soft skills, new companies can't survive, so liberal arts will remain essential in business, legal, medical, and technological communication. So, liberal arts majors, let us know who you are. Tell us about your intellectual passions, and Admissions might just get very excited about you.

NO ACTIVITY BOMBING

It used to be that admissions officers were looking for the Renaissance student, the one who excelled in a little of everything without necessarily concentrating in anything. But that's changed, and these days activity bombing could blow up your application. So don't become involved in four clubs, but do make the *quality* of your involvement in one or two count.

CREATE A UNIQUE NARRATIVE

Don't just be a club member with four or five clubs on your résumé but no leadership. That's activity bombing. Be the person who goes *beyond*. Find the one or two things that really matter to you and build yourself a success story within them. Create a unique narrative.

Admissions officers will see thousands of applications touting the candidate's position as editor-in-chief, debate club leader, or Key Club president. That used to be enough to get you in the door of top colleges, but these titles, although demonstrating school leadership, do not demonstrate the take-charge, entrepreneurial spirit that colleges look for now. Remember that Admissions is hungry for your unique narrative. Ask yourself if being Key Club president will provide Admissions with that narrative. If you've found a passion early in high school, follow it with fervor, hard work, community organizing, and the spirit of leadership. I promise that the journey will bring you unique stories to tell and interesting professionals, from outside the high school community, writing testimonials for you based on the hard work you've put into your life's narrative. Additionally, don't underestimate the importance of telling a personal story of success or failure. Both experiences inform a fascinating college essay, and both build character for life.

So go after that research internship at the hospital; create an app that can help neighborhood nonprofits find donors and volunteers; do outreach to the elderly in your community; organize the schools in your city for a book drive to build libraries in underserved communities; or follow an unusual academic passion, study it overseas in the summer, and write a blog about it. The list of possibilities is never ending, limited only by your imagination. Just be brave and *do something*.

But don't do *everything*. That never works out well—not for you, not for your high school career, and not for your college application.

Now, do not think that your job is done once fall of senior year comes and you have amassed some beautiful awards, a coveted internship, a leadership role, and/or an impressive number of years learning your instrument of choice. Senior year is the time to work on the presentation of these accomplishments. Half the battle in demonstrating that you are a proper match for the college of your choice is being able to show them who you are beyond the list of activities on your résumé. Take time creating a multimedia personal résumé—a living narrative of your high school career. Assemble significant high-definition photos and videos of any successes you've had in high school (athletics, theater, musical performances, debate, science fair poster sessions)—because a visual story of your path is tremendously appealing to Admissions. Admissions officers are so tired of the constant reading of résumés that they find a video or audio format of impressive résumé elements very enticing. Use that to your benefit. We discuss the process of creating this visual résumé, which we call the ResuMotiv™, later on. If you'd like to dig into that now, learn all about it here: www.ResuMotiv.com.

Remember, everything you do to present the authentic and unique academic, creative, and leadership qualities you possess will help Admissions see that they need you on campus! The College Board tells us that only 2 percent of universities reject 75 percent of applicants. Show how special you are, and you'll be on your way to the most exciting and challenging ride of your young life.

REMEMBER THE WHY

In your supplementary essays and additional creative college application materials, remember that the important question to answer is "why" you do what you do. Yes, tell the admissions officers about the "what" you've created and the "how" you've accomplished it, but be sure to tell the "why" as well. "Why" is the most difficult part, yet it tells the most about who you are as a person. It gives us a peek into your character, your motivators, and your convictions. It's what all admissions officers want to determine about their applicants. We'll examine how to mold your "why" into an exceptional essay later in the book.

HUMILITY AND LIKEABILITY

Let's talk for a moment about what *not* to do. When Admissions reads your essay, it doesn't matter how much you've accomplished if you can't write about it humbly. If you don't sound likeable in your profile and essays, you may be staring at the reject pile. It's dangerously easy to come off sounding self-impressed when writing about your accomplishments. Instead, allow those accomplishments to tell their own story, and you'll sound kind, self-motivated, talented, and self-aware. Self-aware is not the same as self-impressed; one suggests that you know yourself and are comfortable in your skin, while the other smacks of egotism. In Chapter Five, we spend quality time discussing how to brag artfully and remain likeable.

CHAPTER THREE

"I WISH I COULD GET MERIT AID..."; YOU CAN!

I f your academics and leadership are exceptional, do apply for the many merit scholarships offered by some of the nation's great universities. The extra applications and accompanying essays for such merit scholarships may pay off big time for you (and sometimes, no extra work is required).

The Ivy League is famous for its generous need-based scholarships, but where can a student go to find great merit-based awards? There are the National Merit Scholarships for those few who receive the title. But how worthwhile is the hunt for universities that offer merit awards? In fact, it can be very worthwhile.

Here is a sample of some eminent and generous merit awards from a handful of our nation's top schools:

At **University of Virginia**, the Jefferson Scholarship provides full tuition and associated costs of attendance at the university for four years. The award is given for demonstrated excellence and potential in the areas of leadership, scholarship, and citizenship. http://www.admission.virginia.edu/scholarships

Vanderbilt University offers the Ingram Scholarship and the Cornelius Vanderbilt Scholarship.

The Ingram Scholarship Program provides full-tuition support each year plus stipends for special summer service projects. The program seeks exceptional academics and social entrepreneurs who will combine a successful business or professional career with a commitment to solving societal problems.

The Cornelius Vanderbilt Scholarship provides full tuition, plus a one-time stipend to be used toward a summer study abroad or research experience after sophomore or junior year. Scholars must maintain a 3.0 GPA. http://www.vanderbilt.edu/scholarships/

Rice University has a lovely way of awarding scholarships: all admitted freshman applicants are automatically considered for merit-based awards, so no separate applications are required. Rice has a number of such awards, including:

- The Trustee Distinguished Scholarship, which is up to $24,000 per year, is given to students whose personal talents have distinguished them among all other applicants.

- The Century Scholars Program, which is $4,000 for each of two years plus a guaranteed research mentorship, is given to those applicants who have distinguished themselves in research.

- The Engineering Scholarship, which can be from $10,000 to full tuition, is for the most exceptional applicants to the Engineering division. http://financialaid.rice.edu/scholarships.aspx

Johns Hopkins has the Hodson Trust Scholarship. It is awarded on the basis of academic and personal achievement, leadership, and contribution and is worth up to $30,500 per year. Fewer than 20 freshmen receive it. Students must maintain a 3.0 GPA on campus. http://pages.jh.edu/~finaid/prosp_stud_scholar.html

UNC-Chapel Hill has the *Morehead-Cain* Scholars Program and the famed Robertson Scholars Leadership Program. Students may not be considered for both scholarships simultaneously, nor can they apply anywhere Early Decision.

Morehead-Cain Scholars who are from out of state are usually nominated by their high schools. The four basic criteria are: scholarship, leadership, character, and physical vigor; it is a highly selective program, and there is a lengthy application with additional essays to complete. As the first merit scholarship program established in the US, the Morehead-Cain provides a full four-year scholarship covering tuition, books, room and board, a laptop computer, and four summer experiences. http://www.moreheadcain.org/

The Robertson Scholars Leadership Program is for dynamic leaders and offers scholars a dual citizenship at UNC and Duke, allowing students to double major and/or take classes at both (while only receiving a diploma from UNC-Chapel Hill): The program provides eight semesters of full tuition, room and board, and mandatory fees at Duke and UNC-Chapel Hill. Scholars also have access to generous funding for up to three summer experiences. http://robertsonschol-ars.org

Cooper Union, an all-honors private college in New York City, gives a great deal of non-need-based aid, with approximately 72 percent of its students receiving merit awards and all incoming students receiving half tuition. Cooper Union provides a rigorous education in architecture, art, or engineering. http://cooper.edu/admissions/tuition-fees

To find the best listings of merit aid data, check out U.S. News College Compass or MeritAid.com, with its well-documented college directories on the topic.

Now, for some of the most sought after merit scholarships and programs that can be won *before* you even become a freshman in college and can open doors for you when Admissions sees them on your application:

National AXA Achievement Scholarship: Exceptional young minds and leaders are awarded for outstanding achievement in school or community. From a pool of 52 state winners, 10 are selected as national winners, receiving $25,000. Special consideration is given to achievements that help society in the fields of education, health, or finance. https://us.axa.com/axa-foundation/AXA-achievement-scholarship.html

Coca-Cola Scholars Foundation: Some of the nation's greatest young minds and leaders are chosen for this scholarship. Highly com-petitive, with thousands applying each year, students complete an application that details their grades and significant leadership inside and outside of school. The 150 selected Coca-Cola Scholars attend Scholars Weekend in April and are awarded $20,000 in scholarship funds: http://www.coca-colascholarsfoundation.org/applicants/#faq

Telluride Association Summer Program (TASP): Although not a cash gift, being accepted into TASP tells Admissions something about your intellect. Students are selected through a competitive application process. TASPers attend a seminar led by university scholars and participate in varied academic (learning for learning's sake) and social activities. TASPers are brought together for a summer of intellectual challenge amid a diverse community of curious minds. It's an honor to be selected. http://www.tellurideassociation.org/programs/high_school_students/tasp/tasp_general_info.html

Research Science Institute (RSI): From June through August annually, 80 of the world's most accomplished high school STEM students attend Massachusetts Institute of Technology (MIT) for the Research Science Institute. Determined through a highly competitive application process, RSI is the most renowned cost-free summer science and engineering program—combining "on-campus course work in scientific theory with off-campus work in science and technology research": http://www.cee.org/research-science-institute

World of Children Award (WOCA): A $25,000 minimum grant for young people who "run sustainable, high-impact programs for children." The WOC Youth Award "recognizes a young person under the age of 21 who has made significant contributions to the lives of other children." http://www.worldofchildren.org/theaward/awards-we-give/youth-award/

National Jefferson Award: Although not a cash award, the National Jefferson Award is our nation's highest public service honor.

A student may win for outstanding national or global service. This student must have committed at a young age to being the change they want to see in their world by starting an organization that makes positive social impact. Young people who receive this award exhibit vision and vow to continue their service efforts. http://www.jeffersonawards.org/national-intro/

Gloria Barron Prize for Young Heroes: The Barron Prize honors 25 inspiring young people who have made a significant positive difference to people and our planet. The top ten winners each receive a $5,000 cash award to support their service work or higher education. http://barronprize.org/

Milton Fisher Scholarship for Innovation & Creativity: Not that many families know about this creative and generous award. Up to $20,000 ($5000 per year for four years of college) is granted to exceptionally innovative and creative high school juniors, seniors, and college freshmen, who may demonstrate their talents in any number of ways. Students must be from Connecticut or the New York City metro area and plan to attend college anywhere in the United States or be from any part of the United States and plan to attend college in Connecticut or New York City. http://www.rbffoundation.org/

Intel International Science and Engineering Fair: The Intel ISEF is "the world's largest international pre-college science competition," with more than 1,700 high school students from over 70 countries, regions, and territories, who showcase their independent research and compete for more than $5 million in prizes. https://student.societyforscience.org/intel-isef.

Siemens Competition in Math, Science, and Technology: The Siemens Competition is "the nation's premiere science research competition for high school students," open to citizens or permanent residents of the United States in their senior year. Students submitting an individual project must be seniors, but team projects may have students in the 9th through 12th grade. Big money can come from being a Siemens winner (up to $100,000), so it's worth investigating. https://siemenscompetition.discoveryeducation.com/about/student-eligibility

• • •

If you're excited by the thought of doing STEM research, contact your high school's research director to learn how to begin the process. Some high schools have Introduction to Research courses; others connect students with labs. However, many schools have neither a research director nor a systematic way of introducing their students to research, and for the students at those schools, I have a special gift for you!

For a free downloadable tip sheet on how to enter and win science fairs, visit www.ScienceFairVideo.com, created for you by College Admission Central's science research director and ISEF-affiliated judge Michael Bluegrass. You'll also learn about the Science Fair Edge™ program, with information on the major science fairs all in one place, along with insight into the kinds of questions the judges ask, the kinds of presentations they expect, the way to begin the process of discovering what area of STEM speaks to you and how to find a mentor in that field.

Although it's difficult to say which awards or honors make the ultimate difference in a top-tier or Ivy League acceptance, any of the above will enrich your lives, grab the attention of Admissions, and move the needle several steps closer.

If you're a STEM-Talented Girl…There's Good News for You

If you're a young woman who's interested in computer science, engineering, and mathematics (as well as the sciences in general) and you have an excellent GPA and strong standardized test scores in math and science…take advantage of the wooing of female STEM applicants going on at our nation's top universities and colleges and apply to them! I am not suggesting that getting into MIT, Cal Tech, Stanford, Harvey Mudd, Yale, Cornell, Carnegie Mellon, Penn, Columbia, or Duke Engineering will be a cakewalk; what I *am* saying is that you will have an advantage. Ride the wave! You've worked hard to demonstrate your talent in these fields; now it's time to take advantage of this trend in elevating female STEM candidates.

Mark Stehlik, assistant dean for undergraduate education at Carnegie Mellon's School of Computer Science, says, "If you are a woman applicant and all things are equal– i.e. if you have exactly the same numerical scores as a man–then it's likely we will vote in your favor because we are committed to diversity." Cornell University College of Engineering presents a dynamic hosting program specifically designed for the class of 2018 female engineers called the Spring Women in Engineering Program (WIE)–an overnight event, focusing on the engineering student experience. At Harvey Mudd College, a school that traditionally had an overwhelmingly male college population, more engineering degrees were awarded to women in May 2014 than to men; 56 percent of graduating engineering students were female, and 44 percent were male. Admission statistics also demonstrate that both MIT and CIT (California Institute of Technology) offer top female applicants interested in engineering and computer science a bump in admission as well

CHAPTER FOUR

YOU, THE EXTRAPRENEUR

"Do I dare / Disturb the universe?"
—T. S. Eliot, "The Love Song of J. Alfred Prufrock"

We've talked a lot about creating opportunities for yourself to find and explore your passions and how that makes you shine. Now let's brainstorm ways to make that happen, no matter where you live, how you're ranked in school, what your personal circumstances may be, and whether or not you've been shut out of the popularity contest that is so often associated with leadership in school.

Being a high school leader starts by thinking like an *extrapreneur*. What does that mean? Well, let's define our terms. First, there's the "entrepreneur"—someone who starts and manages a new business or endeavor, usually with considerable risk and investment. Why is it important for you to know this definition? Because you are moving into an entrepreneurial world.

Then there's the "intrapreneur"—someone who works within the safe, expected confines of an organization to keep the business of the existing organization humming. An intrapreneur would be an in-school leader: president of your class, editor-in-chief of the school newspaper, president of Key Club. All notable and worthwhile leadership positions—but for top colleges, frankly, they're a yawn. They won't come out and say it, but admissions officers at our nation's most esteemed universities are looking for the students who jump the divide and make something happen outside the established adult administrative structure—those who create a company, build a product, advocate for a cause, launch an organization, begin a community project, or take a talent the extra mile. Top-tier schools are looking for those who get an idea and run with it.

In business, those people are called entrepreneurs. In high school, I call them "extrapreneurs," the kids with stars in their eyes who won't take no for an answer even though they're teens. They weigh the possibility of success vs. failure and jump anyway! They are the innovators—they want to see what will happen *if*. They create interesting and worthwhile adventures for themselves in high school and even more interesting college essays. They try, fail, or succeed and write about why they took the journey.

Now, you might be panicked because you're late in getting started. Don't be. There's a track for every motivated student, no matter when you begin to take the reins. An extrapreneur can be born at any moment—and college admissions officers know that, because people awaken at different times in their lives. You might be working a job or taking an entrepreneurship course that turns you on to a specific business idea during the summer before senior year. Even better, you might decide that you should move forward with that idea and start a business during the fall. Imagine the life experience you would garner from drawing up a business plan, organizing friends to help realize it, and having the adventure of succeeding and failing one step at a time as you build the business. Not only are you finding out something authentic about yourself in the process, you are creating a potent narrative for your college personal statement. Nothing wrong with that, is there?

Don't be concerned that the high school "activity bomber" will have it over you in the application process. One leadership endeavor trumps being a professional member. There's much that can be done during the summer before senior year and even during senior year first semester. Let's look at the way a few of my "late bloomers" have gotten themselves noticed by the right college.

Karenna was a solid B student who had not been excited about much until the summer before senior year. When she became concerned about her 13-year-old sister going into the city with friends for a "social life" every couple of weekends, Karenna decided that a real problem in her small town was that it didn't have a safe and "dry" party experience on weekends for middle schoolers. She held a meeting with PTA members and her town mayor and started an old-fashioned ice cream social once a month in the town hall's activity center, with bands from the local middle school playing all evening. She called the event *Middle-Earth*, and it became like an underground, but safe, cult venue in her town. Karenna and a friend would arrange for a different local ice cream shop to be the vendor each month, and students would invite friends from neighboring towns and gather at the social for a retro music and ice cream blowout. *Middle-Earth* was a hit with town businesses, the middle school bands were thrilled because they got to be rock stars every month and invite their friends to hear them perform, and parents loved the idea of their middle school students being safe on the weekend. The PTA even kicked in money toward supplies and cleanup. The biggest winner of all was this "extrapreneurial" student, Karenna, who was written up in her local paper as a hero. By the time the winter rolled around and Karenna had submitted her college applications, she had a hit on her hands. On April 1, Karenna received five out of seven college acceptances she never expected to receive. Ultimately, Admissions were won over by her "extrapreneurial" spirit and the way she made the decisive move to put her actions where her conscience was.

Then there was Gareth. As a sophomore in high school, Gareth caught the acting bug and was cast as the lead in two of his school's productions. He spent the summer before junior year taking voice lessons and going to tap classes in the city. Certainly, this was an enriching experience for Gareth. He was finding his talents. However, there was no particularly pivotal moment in his life yet. After being cast as the lead again during his junior year, Gareth made an unusual decision. He thought ahead to what he might have to do in order to make some money while following this newly found passion for theater.

Voice lessons are expensive, so Gareth decided to become a waiter during the summer leading into senior year. He had a well thought out and rather creative set of reasons for taking this job. Firstly, he wanted to see if he had the disposition to wait tables, as most of the acting students he knew worked at restaurants so they could arrange their shifts around auditions. Secondly, he wanted to pay his own way through voice lessons. But Gareth's third reason was the most fascinating: he decided that if he had to be constantly interacting with strangers while waiting tables, he could use those interactions as opportunities to hone his skill with dialects and accents. Gareth practiced for his daily table-waiting gig by listening to YouTube videos of people speaking in each country's dialects and then pausing the video and working the dialect in front of a mirror. So one day Gareth was from Scotland, the next from England, then France, then Germany. He reran that cycle until he became believable in each accent. It made delivering grilled cheese and coffee a wacky and fun theatrical challenge that Gareth looked forward to each day. Now, that's what I call an authentic narrative!

Gareth found his scholarly side during this intensive summer dialect research project, had a fascinating and unique essay for his Common Application to college, and, by February, had been offered the lead in the national touring company of *Les Miserables*. Gareth, who had floundered through his first two years of high school, gained entrance to Tisch School of the Arts at NYU. The rest is happy college history.

Leila was an accidental late bloomer. Maybe you have a story like hers. Leila was a prolific writer for her school's newspaper. She specialized in interviews with the administration and village officials on topics involving high school policy and technology. Leila was a great student with an A- average, three AP courses on which she scored fives by the end of junior year, and excellent SAT scores. She wasn't one of the popular girls, but she didn't expect popularity to play into whether she would be named the paper's news editor at the end of the year. To make a long story short, the students on the editorial committee had sole responsibility for choosing editors, and they chose someone from their inner circle as news editor. Leila was left without in-school leadership for her college application (and, more upsetting, was humiliated by not having been recognized for her talent and three years of hard work).

A go-getter by nature, Leila decided to move her talents outside the school. By the end of June, she was writing a column about the detrimental effects of the Common Core curriculum on elementary school children for the local paper. By mid-July, Leila had started a blog charging high school students to take up the mantle of leadership outside their school's walls so that their leadership success did not rise and fall on a high school popularity contest and so that students would know what it felt like to be empowered by the time they hit campus. Leila's blog became wildly successful, prompting a call from a marketing and branding company in her city. Impressed by her copywriting skills, the recruiter asked Leila if she would like a summer internship with the firm. Another happy ending.

Leila didn't need that high school editor's title on her college résumé. She was accepted by her top choice Ivy League school, along with four other top-tier colleges. Because Leila took the reins in her life and made something impactful happen, admissions officers noticed her and knew that she would make an impact on their campuses as well. Past success is a powerful predictor of future success. Leila told me that ultimately the most important outcome of this process for her was learning what she was made of, so that she could call upon that strength again in her future professional life.

THAT'S NOT BRILLIANT!

- When you complete only your early application and then wait to see what happens in December before you write your other ten applications over winter break…that's not brilliant!

- When you select English as your major, then tell your interviewer that your favorite books of all time are *The Wolf of Wall Street* and *Batman Vol. 2*…that's not brilliant!

- When you determine that your writing is so exceptional that you can craft your entire personal statement as a flashback or a stream of consciousness…that's not brilliant! (Flashback writing is very difficult to pull off.)

- When you're an average pianist and decide to send in a recording of yourself playing Rachmaninov No. 3…that's not brilliant! (Do you really want to be the applicant whose recording they play at the "After Admission Decision Party," when all the admissions officers are a little tipsy?)

- When you send the admissions officers an additional five recommendations (all of them saying what a smart, talented student you are), just in case they didn't read the previous five…that's not brilliant!

- When it's senior year and you take a long, hard look at your résumé and decide what you really need on there is a nonprofit…so you create a fake one…that's not brilliant! Do you really think admissions officers were born yesterday?

- When you assume that taking the SAT for a fourth time might enhance your chances for admission to Princeton...that's not brilliant! (Taking an SAT more than twice causes concern in Admissions.)

- When you stalk your regional admissions officer so relentlessly that you discover when her birthday is and send her a dozen roses...that's not brilliant! In fact, it's creepy.

- When you write update emails to your admissions officer every two weeks, and your only update is "Just wanted to let you know that X University is still my number one choice"...that's not brilliant!

- When you join six after-school clubs in six different fields of interest, just to have lots of entries on your résumé...that's not brilliant! (That's activity bombing.)

- When you consistently grub for grade changes on exams and papers from a high school teacher and then ask that teacher to write your college recommendation...that's not brilliant! (Somewhere in that recommendation you will be called a "grade grubber." Colleges hate hearing that.)

- When your mom calls Admissions to ask all the questions you should be asking—and you let her...that's not brilliant! (Mom is not going to college—you are! Admissions will make note of these calls.)

- When you have signed in to a college visit welcome book and you leave in the middle of the info session...that's not brilliant!

- When you insult a sector of the population (like corporations or Wall Street) in your essay, just because you're young and idealistic...that's not brilliant! First of all, you don't know who is reading your essay: Perhaps they started their careers on Wall Street, or perhaps their parents are finance professionals. Regardless of how glib, well-researched, or heartfelt your essay, you could be insulting someone. In fact, the people who are endowing your scholarship could have made their livelihoods in the very professions you're berating. If you do feel deeply about a particular issue, write about it in an insightful, balanced, and sensitive way. It never pays to offend.

- When you decide to use your essay as a partisan political platform and decimate the opposing party...that's not brilliant!

- When you receive that early acceptance at your top school and decide to make up for all the missed years of partying by not bothering with homework or studying for exams between January and May...that's not brilliant! (Can you spell "RESCIND"?)

One student, Jonathan, was a first-class tinkerer. He built apps and robotic toys for his cat to chase and took toasters and blenders apart to see if he could combine the parts to create new kitchen appliances. He loved building things but realized there were greater purposes for his talents. Thank goodness for college applications, because those gave him the kick that he needed to do something truly impactful.

Jonathan planned on studying engineering at a top college, but, being from a big East Coast city, he knew he had to distinguish himself so that he'd pop off the pages of his application. That's all the impetus Jonathan needed to begin an engineering project for social good.

Soapbox car racing was a popular activity in Jonathan's hilly neighborhood, but he had never made the time to actually build his own. Relying only on gravity to run, a winning soapbox car is an impressive creation—and even more impressive when the car is racing to fund a pet visitation program at the local children's hospital. Jonathan's idea was to organize a small derby and have each competitor ask schoolmates, friends, and relatives from their own part of the city to make a donation by sponsoring the competitor's car in the race. Not only would Jonathan be able to show his building prowess; he would demonstrate what a fine community organizer he was as well.

After months of rallying like-minded and talented friends, six snazzy looking cars had been built, using standardized wheels with precision ball bearings. The competitors began their descent from a ramp on top of the neighborhood's highest hill and reached speeds of 35 miles per hour. The beautiful end to this story is that there was no loser. Every one of the six young engineers had raised money for the pet program so that, taken together, Jonathan's derby raised $5,600. Two months later, Jonathan and his five friends walked into the children's hospital to inspect the realization of their vision. There in the playroom were two collies, a St. Bernard, and a beagle surrounded by seven children in need of a fluffy distraction and a little love.

Now, that's the way to use your college application experience to find out what you're made of for life. Don't stress, even if you feel like you're getting a late start. It's a big world, and what you do can make a difference for the better—and, in the process, favorably impress Admissions with your imagination and entrepreneurial energy.

For those of you who would like to try your hand at being entrepreneurial (or extrapreneurial!) but don't know where to begin, try contacting the Young Entrepreneurs Academy (YEA!). YEA! is a rather revolutionary program that teaches students in grades 6 through 12 about the process of starting and running a business. The program mentors these students throughout the academic year. Students work collaboratively with local business leaders, community representatives, and educators to develop their ideas and goals, create business plans, "pitch" potential investors, obtain funding, register with governmental agencies, develop their brand identity, and more. Call 585-272-3535 or email info@yeausa.org.

Six Steps to Bringing YEA! to Your School:

1. Introduce the academy to your school's superintendent and principal.

2. Introduce the academy to the board of directors of your local chamber of commerce.

3. Complete the YEA! program adoption agreement.

4. Receive YEA! materials, and staff your local class.

5. Receive comprehensive training from YEA!

6. Launch your academy.

CHAPTER FIVE

YOU, GIFTED

If you're blessed with a special ability or an out-of-the-box interest, that's great—but as is true in all of life, it's what you do with it that counts. You need to be especially creative in finding ways to explore your strengths and, at admissions time, to showcase your gifts and how you've used them.

Let's talk about two students I worked with, Andrew and Katya. Andrew was a talented filmmaker, Katya an extraordinary cellist. At the outset, this sounds like two separate stories—but it's not. Both students required parental and guidance counselor advocacy, both needed to create multimedia résumés or portfolios of their work during high school in order to gain access to the right artistic enrichment programs, and both emerged as stars amid their high school applicant pool wherever they applied.

Did Andrew or Katya have the highest GPAs or standardized test scores in their class? No, they did not. They were excellent students who took rigorous high school course schedules—but so did all the other excellent students in their class. So what made admissions officers at Princeton, Yale, Columbia, Stanford, University of Chicago, and Northwestern take notice and accept them? Andrew and Katya had studied and pursued their passions and talents at weekend conservatory programs. They dealt with the artistic rigors, stresses, and high performance required by two schools simultaneously. They sought to become accomplished in their arts—and that made them very interesting applicants.

By sophomore year in high school, Andrew had a compelling reel of short films that he had written, directed, and produced. He attended a Saturday film program at a noted film school in his city. In the spring of sophomore year, Andrew and his parents made an appointment with Andrew's guidance counselor to discuss a split high school schedule for junior year—mornings at his public high school (taking honors and AP courses) and afternoons at film school. Because of his well-organized and creative reel, and a history of his passion for and involvement in film, Andrew's guidance counselor pled his case to the school's administrative directors, and they allowed Andrew to compact his academic schedule. This high school made a smart move: by investing in Andrew's talents, they assured he would be a stand-out in the college admissions pool—not only because of the level of film work he could produce and submit to colleges but because he would be able to demonstrate a serious thread of passion throughout his high school years.

A New York City resident, Katya had studied cello privately since the age of five. By 8th grade, Katya's technique and repertoire were so advanced that she knew she was ready for conservatory. However, Katya was also a strong academic student and didn't think it was the right move, personally, to spend her entire high school career in conservatory. After a little research, Katya learned what repertoire she needed to perfect for auditions to Manhattan School of Music's and Juilliard's Saturday precollege programs. She practiced three hours a day all through 8th grade. By spring, she was ready. Thinking ahead, she videotaped her final practice so that she would have proof of her hard work for future auditions and her precollege record; then she took her auditions. Katya was admitted on scholarship to Manhattan School of Music's Saturday conservatory program. She would now get the chance to work with her teacher of choice.

Because she was smart enough to make the videotape, she had it as an advocacy tool in her sophomore year of high school, when she needed to ask permission of her guidance office to leave school early two days a week for extra lessons in the city as she prepared for national competitions. Without proof of her talent and dedication, along with her attendance at a world-renowned Saturday conservatory program, Katya's high school administration would not have agreed to compact her schedule so that she could leave for rehearsals and lessons. End result: Both Andrew and Katya were accepted at their colleges of choice—at both Ivy League and top conservatory programs. This is advice that you can take or leave, but I hope that you get the chance in your high school career to take it.

A Love Letter to the Stage—and why you should grab the chance to be a part of your high school's theater program.

I've always believed that every student—the quirky, the average, the athletic, the introverted, the life of the party, the super industrious, and the super intellectual—should have an experience alongside the super talented on stage. Every student should take the opportunity to be in a high school show.

Theater teaches us most of what we need to be successful in life:

Be kind to everyone, from your director to the stagehand to the lighting designer to the walk-on. Your performance—however small or large—is dependent on these people; and although you may be a lead now, the guys in the chorus might be waving at you in a year or two on their way up.

Learn your lines. If you don't do your homework, study, and rehearse to the best of your ability, you won't be in any shape to put in a good performance—that goes for onstage, in the classroom, in the boardroom, or in the operating room.

Learn to improvise. When something goes wrong onstage you have only moments to fix it, so you had better learn to be fast on your feet. We rarely think about this, but if an actor drops a prop and doesn't find a way to improvise and pick it up, no matter how extraordinary his performance is after that drop, no one is paying attention. All anyone in the audience is thinking about is when and how he's going to pick up that prop. In school, at work, in relationships…things will go wrong. You can either learn how to pivot quickly and fix them, or you can let the errors define you.

Learn to connect. Connecting with an audience from the stage is a subtle art—the same art that enables you to cultivate new friends at college or convince a company that you're an excellent internship candidate. It's one part communicating confidence in who you are (a quality that inspires people to get behind you as a leader), one part allowing some vulnerability to show, one part being aware of how to "read" your surroundings (that is, to know your audience), and one part likeability. If you can connect, you can persuade. If you can persuade, you can make big things happen in your life—including persuading admissions at a few of your dream colleges that you will make their campus more interesting and colorful with your presence.

Be microcommitted. When you're onstage you can have only one focus... your performance. Are you in the moment? Are you reacting authentically to your castmates? Are you remaining in character? Nothing else going on in the environment matters—not the coughing man in the audience stage right, not the chattering little girl stage left, not the woman texting about the performance in center orchestra, and not the latecomer who can easily throw you off your game. Your commitment to this one small task on this one small stage is the thing that makes the difference in how your audience will perceive your talent. It might get you a great review in the school newspaper, it might be the beginning of a shining career, or it might just give you the confidence to know that you can handle being in front of an audience of hundreds. So don't be afraid of making microcommitments. You make one in school when you focus on studying for one standardized test and bow out of the social scene for a month or two while you prepare; you make one when you start brainstorming your personal statement for college—draft after draft until that one essay is the best creative writing you have ever done; you make one when you compete with your team for the title in a national debate, cross-country race, or DECA competition; you make one when you decide that science research is the thing you want to explore and the place you want to excel, so you spend a year of your life on original research that *might* get you to Intel ISEF; you make one when you decide that there is something glorious in you and you're going to share it with the world by getting a community service or entrepreneurial project off the ground—regardless of how much time and energy this *one* project will take to launch. Making these meaningful microcommitments throughout high school will not only teach you what you're made of but will undoubtedly catch the eye of admissions officers at the colleges you dream about. The little things can become the biggest catalysts in our lives…because little hinges swing big doors.

Moral of the story: if you have a special gift or talent, take the early years of your life to train, rehearse, perform, create, produce—and then keep an organized record of your accomplishments. Search for after-school and weekend programs at the highest level, then audition for them. Keep a video library or portfolio of all your best work. Then, by sophomore year of high school, when you've acclimated to the new level of academic work required in your courses, advocate for a compacted schedule at school so that you can further elevate your talents and skills during the school week by attending a professional school or conservatory part time. Keep your grades high, take as many AP or IB courses as is comfortable before leaving for your arts program, and arrange to take any remaining courses that don't fit into your morning schedule on a homeschool basis. You will find that when the time comes to apply to college, your admissions portfolio will be richer and more interesting than the students in your class who have done straight academics, or ten APs, and in-school leadership. You will stand out as the special catch! Don't be afraid to be different. It comes naturally to you, if you let it.

THE GIFTED ATHLETE

The gifted student athlete's application also requires special attention in order to make the best impression on Admissions. These are the steps every serious student athlete should take when applying to college:

- **Be sure about the level at which you want to play in college.** It's a huge commitment to accept recruitment to a school. Are you okay with spending most of your non-class time with a coach and teammates? Will you have enough time to study, keep up a solid GPA, and stay engaged in classes? Most of your college time as a recruit will not be your own: Is that okay with you?

- **As a freshman, get the NCAA worksheets from your guidance counselor** (in the *Guide for the College-Bound Student-Athlete* from http://www. ncaapublications.com) to keep track of your course and grade information.

- **Understand that the NCAA looks at your GPA in core courses only.** Remember that the more rigorous the course load, the better for you in the eyes of admissions committees. So if you've got what it takes to be recruited and also have a fairly rigorous academic schedule of honors and AP courses, you become a very attractive candidate. Don't focus your high school career entirely on a sport without paying serious attention to your academics. That all-or-nothing attitude might hurt you in the end.

- **Contact the athletic departments of the schools you are most interested in.** Ask for preliminary information and the email address for the coach (which you can usually find online with a little research). You cannot wait for college coaches to find you. Be proactive. In fact, if you have the video clips, talent, and "numbers" to reach out to college coaches at the end of sophomore year…do it. Remember, college coaches are not allowed to write to you directly until junior year, so go ahead and make first contact. The coaches, if interested, will then reach out to your high school coach for further information.

- **Make sure your coach has the latest information from the three largest athletic conferences**—the National Collegiate Athletic Association (NCAA), the National Association of Intercollegiate Athletics (NAIA), and the National Junior College Athletic Association (NJCAA).

- **When you're ready to make contact**, gather some high-definition video and significant photos of yourself in action and use them to create an impressive multimedia résumé to send to college coaches while you are in sophomore or junior year. No need to wait until you're a senior.

- **Spend a summer at sports camp.** If your top college choice runs a summer sports program, it would be wise to spend your summer there. This is a way for the college coach to observe your skills and for you to get a feel of the campus.

- **For those who hope to play Division I or II, register with the NCAA eligibility center.**

- **Demonstrate early interest in colleges you have identified as good fits by sending letters to the admissions office.** You should send these by spring of junior year, at the latest. For Division III, you can send emails of demonstrated interest directly to the college coach in the early fall of senior year and still get a response. Often, the coach will check with the admissions office about your academic standing (if you're a senior) before getting back to you, so you might receive a hint as to whether you have a favorable admissions profile from the coach's email response.

- **Submit a separate athletic résumé.** Along with the important student academic record and basic school information, you must also include sports statistics from ninth grade through senior year.

- **Submit a highlight video of five to ten minutes that demonstrates your athletic prowess during a crucial portion of a game.** From this video, the coach may make the decision to come watch you play at a game or invite you to meet at the college.

An excellent source for college athletic recruitment details is The College Athletic Recruiting Process: http://www.laxpower. com/recruits/Hopkins_Recruiting_Guide.pdf

CHAPTER SIX

ACING YOUR ESSAY; HOW TO MAKE YOUR WRITING STAND OUT

Freshmen, Sophomores, and Juniors, *do not* skip over the advice below just because you haven't yet come to the "essay" part of applying to college. Please study this chapter, because what you do in your first three years of high school will create the experiences you will be writing about in your senior year!

You know how you think you should wait until inspiration strikes before digging into your college essay? *Don't.* Make inspiration happen. As William Butler Yeats said, "Do not wait to strike till the iron is hot; but make it hot by striking."

Finding that one focused thought, that special characteristic you possess that makes you an interesting human being or a memorable roommate, that thread of passion, that course or teacher for whom you're excited to wake up in the morning—that is a journey traveled via stories. Telling a story that reflects well on you without coming off as bigheaded requires a light touch we call artful bragging.

When one student, Marco, and I began our discussion for one of his essays about something that inspired him, we went through all the usual suspects: special summer programs that might have lit a fire under him, club leadership, starting a community project, a business, a travel experience, a sport, or a talent... Finally, I queried, "So if it's not an extracurricular program in school that makes you joyous about attending school each day, is it a class?"

"No," responded Marco, "It's a teacher. I've had the amazing luck of having the same English teacher, Mr. Harlow, for two years: Honors and AP English Language and Composition. Not only has he been an inspiration in the classroom, but he has been a mentor and a larger-than-life character I'll never forget."

"If you can reveal something meaningful about yourself that you have discovered and acted upon based on that mentorship, then that's your essay!" I responded. It turns out that Marco hadn't realized just how inspired he had been by his quirky but innovative high school English teacher. You see, as part of Marco's community service work, he taught English grammar to an inner city group of middle school students every weekend, and he had borrowed Mr. Harlow's unusual and entertaining techniques. It turns out that Marco's students returned the love by scoring well on his tests.

Once he'd identified the subject for his essay, Marco wrote his first draft within an hour, and it started with the following unusual conversation:

I walked into the classroom and saw Mr. Harlow, head down and buried in piles of papers, happily commenting, unpacking quotes, and spearing arguments. His beard looked particularly glorious that day. It was an anti-war protester kind of beard...a fervently democratic beard!

"I am assuming you are here on top secret business?" Mr. Harlow asked, peering up at me.

"Yes," I replied as I walked past the cast bronze sculpture of Dr. Freud on Mr. Harlow's windowsill.

"Take a seat and give me your problems, Marco," Mr. Harlow always said that as if his room was the literary confession chamber of the Vatican—soon all of my questions about his assignment would be clarified.

I asked for elucidation on a line of argument brought up by an author we were reading.

"For this, young Marco, we must consult the Doctor. I'll just be a minute," Mr. Harlow replied smiling.

Mr. Harlow then turned and engaged the sculpted head of Freud in meaningful conversation about my question. This is how all the major rulings in our English classes were decided. I never understood a single word Harlow said while he was speaking to the Doctor in German, but it was entertaining—like watching a method actor getting into character. I was rapt. This was the kind of educator I wanted to become—captain of a larger-than-life classroom. I sharpened my teaching skills and creativity every Saturday at the middle school grammar extra-help program in the heart of the city."

Marco's essay poured from him after our creative brainstorming session. The piece uncovered the authentic, energetic personality of an intellectually curious young student with a big personality and the heart of a future educator. Admissions loved the essay because Marco had not been afraid to show his quirky side. Marco's subsequent colorful description of how he, himself, taught and motivated other young lives, having been inspired by his own teacher, made for a moving and successful personal statement.

Students should never be afraid of the color and quirkiness of a potential essay. Sometimes, we can learn the most about you from your sense of humor or adventure. Let's take the case of Tony. A son of two parents who had arrived in the United States from Cuba as teenagers, Tony was devoted to doing his community service at a Latino senior center in his city. When Tony and I began speaking about personal statement topics, his stories always returned to the senior center. One woman, Marta, who particularly endeared herself to Tony, said that the thing she missed most in life was salsa dancing. Tony made a promise to himself to learn how to salsa and decided to bring a recording to the center and dance with Marta on her birthday. But where was he going to find someone to teach him? Neither his mother nor father had learned the moves. He would ask his AP Spanish teacher, Señor Perico—the go-to guy for everything Latino: samba, mambo, salsa, and every cultural ingredient in between. Tony set up his essay's first paragraph with tremendous flair, finishing the piece with his heartwarming dance with Marta on her special day. Here's a peek at the first paragraph:

"Señor Perico, our fashion-forward AP Spanish teacher who hailed from the culturally rich streets of Puerto Rico, made class like a fiesta every day. We listened to reggaeton and salsa, danced like natives of Old San Juan, and spoke about Spanish soap operas. It was his way of wrapping us in heritage. The girls loved him because he wore purple shirts with matching patterned socks, and the boys admired him because all the girls loved him. Señor Perico had a flair for the dramatic—he never whispered when he could emote and never explained when he could thrill. Just the man for the job I had in store. Salsa is not on the AP curriculum, but I had a promise to keep, and Señor Perico would help me keep it. Twice a week for a half hour after extra help, I came for my lesson: how to lead by giving claves, how to dance 'on 2,' the cross-body lead, the open break, and multifarious turns and tricks of the art form. Students who passed by the study center thought we had lost our minds, but Marta would be so proud of me."

MAKE IT PERSONAL–BUT DON'T OVERSHARE

Once upon a time there was a boy named Kurt who shared too much. Kurt was victim to a generation that tells us via Twitter, Facebook, Pinterest, and Instagram where they went for lunch, ice cream, dinner, and moment to moment socializing—accompanied by hourly photos and updates of whom they were with at each location.

We live in a potent sharing force field where young people are drawn as much to each other's tragedies as they are to friends' lunch and college choices. Why is this a problem? Because these same high school seniors extend the sharing to their college essays.

Let's take the case of Kurt. Kurt is a good student but a bit volatile. When his girlfriend broke up with him sophomore year, Kurt cut third period and stopped studying for a week, causing an unfortunate dip in his grades for that quarter. When Kurt's coach benched him one Saturday because his game was off, Kurt didn't show up to practice for the next week and missed a game. *That'll show the coach*, he thought.

During junior year, Kurt recognized his anger issues and over-reactions and worked hard to rein them in to keep balance in his academic and social life. He reached a 3.85 in his GPA. Proud of this journey, Kurt wrote a first draft personal statement about overcoming his past volatility.

We didn't green-light the essay.

We explained to Kurt that, although it was admirable that he was now facing his demons and winning, the portrait his essay painted was of an unbalanced young man who might snap at college when faced with too much stress or disappointment—socially or academically. Although it can be compelling to write about a frailty or obstacle one has faced and risen above, emotional obstacles are better left within the loving circles of family and counselors. Admissions will just see a red flag if your past trials hint at emotional instability. Admissions officers are very careful to admit only students they think can handle the intellectual rigors of their courses and the emotional challenges of living away from home. If you have won the battle with your personal demons—bravo to you! But please understand that there is no need to share that with complete strangers who hold your academic future in their hands, because they may only remember the problem when deciding to accept or reject, not the victory.

WHAT ADMISSIONS OFFICERS SAY THEY WANT AND WHAT THEY REALLY WANT...

Admissions officers say they look for the student's unique voice in each essay, but you had also better send sophisticated writing on non-trite subjects. Remember, you're writing on a college level now, not to your friend from camp. So...

- No contractions.

- No trite essay topics like "How I Made It through Outward Bound," "How I Scored the Winning Touchdown," or "How I Saved the World with My Community Service Trip."

- No colloquial speech—your writing has to pass muster in a top college classroom. If it's too cutesy or informal, it may not bring you an acceptance letter.

Stephen Farmer, associate provost and director of undergraduate admissions at the University of North Carolina-Chapel Hill said, "What we want for students is the feeling that they're looking for the next great thing they need to know. We like to see a sense of joy and curiosity."

You may say you're just a regular kid, who hasn't traveled, founded an organization, built a robot, won national competitions, or held an internship in Silicon Valley. Okay, but drill down to find out what makes you tick. Do you love visiting with your grandparents on the weekend? Why? Tell us in detail. What does that say about you? Do you feel strongly about making your own money and that's why you have a job after school? Why? Where will that attitude take you in life? It doesn't matter if that job is at a New York law firm, a Los Angeles film editing company, or your corner drugstore. The reason for doing that job every day and taking pride in having it is a story in itself.

- Are your parents immigrants? How has that affected what you want from life? What do they expect from you, and what do you want for yourself? How will this make you different from others on campus? Why is that part of the fabric of who you are?

- Have you ever engaged in an activity that changed your point of view?

- Do you read the paper each day? If so, why is that important, and what does it say about you?

- Have you always wanted to do something but haven't yet? What has stopped you? Are you planning on doing it? What do you expect to get out of that experience? Why do you want it?

- Are you a sports enthusiast who always attends your friend's piano recitals? Why is that important to you? What do you take away from those recitals? What does it say about the kind of friend you are, the kind of outside interests you follow, or your intellectual curiosity?

Thoughtful, well-crafted answers to any of these questions will paint a picture of you and the kind of student you'll be on campus. Don't worry that you don't have the proper tools or interesting experiences needed to tell your own story. You've got plenty!

> *"Most of the basic material a writer works with is*
> *acquired before the age of fifteen."*
> —*Willa Cather*

For more insights and strategy on creating your unique and compelling essay, I invite you to visit www.EssaySuite.com.

CHAPTER SEVEN

ACING YOUR APPLICATIONS: HOW TO JUMP OFF THE PAGE AND INTO THE ACCEPTANCE PILE

The perfect chance for you to use your artful bragging skills is on the Common Application. There are myriad opportunities for you to shine in crafting the answers, long or short, to the questions you'll be asked to consider. The Common Application is not as daunting if you take the time to think through what the admissions officers are looking for behind the rather generic questions and then tell your story with a lot of color, detail, authenticity, and a little vulnerability.

For the main essay, there are five options to choose from, and there will often be supplementary essays for each of your schools. The Common Application essay options are:

- Your personal background story

- How you learned from a failure

- How you challenged a belief or idea

- An ideal place you experienced

- An experience that marked your transition to adulthood

The right essay to choose is the one that jumps out and speaks to you. The "failure" essay can be compelling but only if you can write about how you created a success out of that failure or have shown significant development as a human being from that failing. If the failure is going to cast a bad light on you as a student or person, *do not choose it.*

Remember not to rehash the main theme of your application. What does that mean? If you're an award-winning scientist, we don't necessarily want to read an essay about your science, unless it takes us on a journey. If the essay repeats your résumé or the main thread of your application, you could be viewed as one-dimensional. We want to see you as a person; a leader, a friend, a philosopher, an academic (in a different way, perhaps, from what your application conveys), a passionate explorer of something! The essay is a personal statement, not a five-paragraph analysis for English class. It's a story. Tell it colorfully and compellingly, and you'll win.

THE PERSONAL STATEMENT: WHAT DO ADMISSIONS OFFICERS CARE ABOUT?

Admissions officers care about the little things you've done that show character. For example, let's say you have a proclivity for archery but never had a place to practice, so when your brother got you a bow and arrow when you were eight, you'd run down to the lake every day after school and practice hitting cans. All you wanted to do was hit the can down the center. You would stay in one spot for hours until you did it. You may not think this says much, but it shows focus and stick-to-itiveness from an early age. Past attention to detail bodes well for a college career.

Admissions cares that:

- You're a writer who finds the greatest inspiration while kayaking, so you do that every weekend, and, after pulling your boat back onto the shore, you take out your journal and write another short story (that's how you've written enough to publish your first book).

- The first thing that ever inspired you to compose a cello sonata was hearing mourning doves outside your window each day, so you crafted your piece to echo the sounds they left in your memory.

- You're an Anglophile and saved your babysitting money for four years so that you could spend the summer interning with a parliamentary official in London.

- You are an eternal student, and that's why you've chosen to spend the last three summers studying in ways you'd never be able to in high school in the United States— like French art at the Sorbonne, English history at Oxford, or German language in Berlin.

Perhaps you are a varsity swimmer who wanted to have a deeper experience with the ocean and went off to do marine research in St. Croix—diving to spear the invasive lionfish. Or maybe you're a dreamer from a small town who never had the money to travel but always yearned to study the classics with the greatest scholars in the field, and until that day comes, you spend your time on weekends lost among the library stacks in your small town, reading about Zeus, Heracles, and Triton.

Maybe you spent your childhood taking in the kittens that nobody wanted (this says a great deal about your nature). Maybe you were a student who got bullied throughout middle school for not being articulate, then went on to become a TEDx presenter about bullying. I worked with one student who was fascinated by educational psychology and got a learning disabled child to say the alphabet by ballroom dancing with her every day after school. Another student of mine, a high school senior, bought a used car with his birthday money and began a grocery delivery service for senior citizens in his community—now with 100 drivers.

Maybe you were the little girl who used to climb outside her upstairs bedroom window each evening to read quietly on her roof while her brother practiced the trumpet—and grew up to collect donations of enough books to fill 57 new libraries in Ghana, Kenya, and Togo. Or the boy whose weekly visits with his artistic grandma taught him to become an expert on Chagall.

Any of these is the stuff of a great compelling personal essay. You, too, have had special life experiences that can open a window onto your essence and inspire an admissions officer to champion your application in committee meetings.

Remember—tell *your* story, not the story others may advise you to tell. In some schools, like the University of Chicago, 30–50 percent of acceptance decisions are based on the essay. With students being well trained these days in the science of taking standardized exams and high school grading systems being so different (with one high school's A+ being another high school's A-), the authentic voice in the essay and the teacher recommendations have become the highest priorities in admittance. "The very best essays come from students who have devoted a significant amount of time to introspection and preparation. It is apparent to us when a student has spent only a couple hours on an essay," Garrett Brinker, senior assistant director of admissions at the University of Chicago, was quoted as saying.

Clearly the college personal statement isn't something you want to do over a weekend. Not only will this important essay take hours to write the first time, but to make your story the most polished it can be, you will want to edit the piece several times, especially if you are to properly distill your message into the application's word counter: "Not that the story need be long, but it will take a long while to make it short," as Henry David Thoreau said. Every school is looking for students who can write cogently and compellingly—even for STEM students, the ability to communicate clearly is key.

Now, there is always a student who is driven to write about a topic that is either obscure or hotly political. Here is my advice: by all means write about the esoteric, if that's what makes you who you are. However, be sure to provide excellent factual background and content for the admissions officer, because not everyone is as plugged into your topic of interest as you are. If you give colorful detail, you may just inspire a new enthusiast. For the political zealots among you, feel free to write about the political issues that stir your pot, but do so with care, facts, sober judgment, and awareness that the possibility of inciting an admissions officer's ire might not be worth the subject choice. Religion and politics remain tough sells in a personal statement.

You'll notice that I consistently call this major Common Application essay the personal statement. That is because this piece, above all others that you may write for supplements, is expected to shine a light on the unique human being who is seeking a place at the university. Admissions officers want to know, "How will this student make the classroom more intriguing? How will this student use the rich facilities of our campus clubs and publications? How will this student make the most of our investment in them?

Amy Jarich, UC Berkeley's assistant vice chancellor and director of undergraduate admissions, agrees that students should think of these as personal statements rather than essays. A truly personal statement will present a clear view into your intellectual passions, your inquisitiveness, your motivators, and your character. Write an intimate presentation of who you are—not the person you think Admissions wants to meet.

"Begin with an individual, and before you know it you have created a type; begin with a type, and you find you have created—nothing."
—*F. Scott Fitzgerald*

And don't forget to keep your bragging artful, not boastful. Yes, you must tell the admissions officer about the thriving organization or business you started, but add a touch of humility to a sentence here and there, like "and I feel privileged to have had the experience" or "it was an extraordinary yet humbling experience to watch as my organization reached those heights." Be sure to explain how it made you feel and why you began the project in the first place. While you're telling us the "why," we will notice your qualities of passion, leadership, and curiosity; your desire to reach out to the neighborhood or global community; or your intent to do positive work in your field of interest.

Do brag about the leading roles you received in theater since freshman year, but then explain what it meant to you to be on that stage in that capacity. Perhaps you began classical voice lessons at age twelve and have already been accepted to a weekend conservatory program. Tell us why you worked so hard and why you chose that focus so early. Then segue to the leading role on stage in high school, and tell us about your enthusiasm for continuing your art on the college campus. In this way, you have appropriately "bragged."

It is your right to do this bragging in your college essays, because your college will want to brag about you in the future. No one can express the special things you have accomplished in your short life on this earth as well as you. It is your voice that provides us with the "why." Will it feel like you are selling yourself? Perhaps, but people spend their lives selling who they are in one way or another. It's the spirit with which you present your talents and intellect that is the most powerful vehicle for acceptance—whether in college, in the workplace, on stage, or in your social circles.

Pay careful attention to how the students who wrote the following essays "sell" themselves. You will notice a gentle pullback from full-out bragging through elements like humor, expressed vulnerability, surprise, a statement about their passion, a love of an academic course of study, or straight factual scientific writing that impresses less through its creative language than through the well-informed research.

In this first short segment, we learn about a successful entrepreneurial student's love of history and business and how he connected to both passions on the banks of Venice one summer (please keep in mind that his résumé discusses his business ventures to date):

> "*This past summer, I experienced an 'out of book' connection to places that breathed and pulsed with the energy of a field in which I have experienced success and intend to pursue. On the docks of the port city of Venice, I stood and watched as the longshoreman tied rope to cleat and was overcome by the knowledge that where I was standing had been a place in which the spirit of organized international trade had burgeoned and thrived. I thought about the Bills of Exchange that passed from hand to hand during the loading and unloading of a galleon laden with silk. Here I was at one of the great centers in which banking and international trade flourished on a grand scale. I felt humbled, and yet overwhelmingly connected to the business innovators of the day, and what washed over me were the questions, 'How would I innovate?' 'What would be my legacy?'*"

From this elegant paragraph, the student shows us that he is both thoughtful and eager to leave his mark on the world.

Another artful opening—this one from a young engineer's personal statement:

> "*When I was seven I had a Nerf gun that shot foam darts, propelled out of a tube by a jet of air—but I was disappointed that they didn't shoot further, straighter, and faster. I was determined to discover what created the air pressure and what factors influenced the trajectory of the darts. I noticed restrictions in the airway path and wondered if they were placed intentionally to degrade the performance, and if so,*

why? I set up a work station in my basement and notated each alteration and accompanying result, removed the restrictive little baffles, shortened and alternately lengthened the nozzle to change its characteristics, reassembled the toy and created a testing range to measure its new flight characteristics. Although I wasn't able to answer all of my questions through inspection, experimentation and my limited kid resources, I felt fulfilled by the quest. Now I work with bigger toys."

Simple, yet captivating, because we learn something about the development of this young, talented engineer, who later in the essay describes the project that ultimately brought him to a winning place in Intel ISEF. There's nothing inauthentic or off-putting about an essay like this—the student simply took a specific fond, hands-on memory and brought us from the past into his present world of academic and technical success in engineering.

What to Do and What Not to Do for a Winning "Why" Essay...

When colleges or universities ask why you want to attend, they expect detailed answers. In fact, your "Why X University" essay can make or break your chance for admittance.

- Don't include generic paragraphs that could be switched out for another school.

- Don't take entire essays and simply change names of departments and courses that you'd like to take.

- Don't discuss climate or the beauty of the campus.

- Do speak about specific professors with whom you'd like to study or do research.

- Do speak about what you intend to study (it's okay; admissions officers know that this can change during college) and what you hope to take from and give to that campus, both academically and in your extracurricular pursuits.

Admissions can tell when their school's "why" essay has been put together with broadly worded puzzle pieces from other schools' "why" essays. Your job is to make every college feel loved and special—not generic. Prove, point for point, how X University will fulfill your collegiate academic and extracurricular vision. Do not just say that X University has a good major in politics. Explain why the school's particular major is well suited to you. Which courses are you excited about taking? Is there an interdisciplinary spirit to the department that fits your broad way of looking at the world? Is there a professor with whom you'd like to do research? Why? Who are the professors whose classes you're excited about taking? Which clubs or publications do you wish to become involved with and why?

NAILING THE "WHY"

An example of a weak "why" essay:

"I am interested in many subjects, and I know I will be happy academically at Tulane University because it has a broad selection of courses. I can major in business and still take English and history. This is important to me because I am still deciding on my major. I have been inspired to study courses across many disciplines and have become active in lots of school activities like the newspaper and Key Club. I expect to be involved in many activities on campus as well, and in that way, give back to my school."

Well meaning, but unacceptable. The first problem with this "why" paragraph is that it doesn't tell us *why* anything! Additionally, almost every sentence starts with "I." Repetition of the same word or pronoun from sentence to sentence makes the writing uninteresting and repetitive.

Another flaw is the general and weak substantiation of points. This essay, above all, must provide the details of what makes this particular university the right fit for you—according to the high school courses you've taken and loved, according to the opinions you hold about political or social matters, according to the career path you hope to pursue, according to the talents you wish to develop, and so on. Details, details, details. Show how much due diligence you put into your research for every university to which you apply. Not only aren't there specific courses or professors provided in the paragraph above, but we are not at all sure that this applicant has written the "why" paragraph for this specific university. Replace Tulane with the name of another university and see if it fits just as well. Unfortunately for this student, it does.

An Example of a Good "Why" Essay

> *"...I am attracted to Carnegie Mellon's EHPP major, Ethics, History & Public Policy, which ties together history, society, and policy through courses in political philosophy, American and European history, ethics, and foundations of law, while preparing students for leadership. What an appealing course of study for a dedicated student of history and political science with an intellectual curiosity about political philosophy and ethics! Carnegie Mellon continues to impress me with the real-world approach in its Washington Semester Program, allowing students to study public policy and intern with leaders in the political and business realms for one semester. It is a testament to this real-world awareness that the Division of Student Affairs at Carnegie Mellon offers workshops in and opportunities for developing leadership skills—encouraging students to reflect on the substance and weight of leadership on campus and in the world. With my emerging work as a national speaker in government regulation of business, such workshops and campus opportunities for 'leadership learning' will be invaluable to me."*

This is an excerpt from a well-researched and substantial "why" essay. The segment explains in detail how a number of programs offered by CMU would be of great value and interest in shaping the student's intellectual and career paths. The student goes on later to explain how he would give back to the university through enthusiastic membership in various clubs and publications.

A FEW SAMPLE SEGMENTS FROM DIFFERENT TYPES OF ESSAYS

Let's look at an example of artful bragging—this time, in the form of a short activity essay:

"This past summer during my research at XYZ Medical School, I became curious about a list of SNPs likely linked to MS. My eye was drawn towards a SNP relatively low on the list, which had been all but ignored by the analysts in favor of old standbys like IL-6 or CD58. The gene was ITGB4, which codes for the beta-4 strand of á-6-β-4 integrin, an extracellular signaling protein I knew to have receptors in the adhesive protein laminin. Laminin is an instrumental element in the signaling cascade that leads to activation of oligodendrocytes and subsequent myelination of MS-affected regions. I followed my hunch with extensive reading and led the lab to consider that it may be the first gene to act both as a protection from autoimmunity and as a facilitator of myelination. Because of my investigations, ITGB4 and its role in MS will now be explored further by way of an Affy gene chip. My curiosity led to my being credited for having significantly impacted two major laboratory publications."

Excellent. This young researcher gives the facts in the language of his field, showing that he has mastery over what he studied; he plainly expresses how his curiosity led to two laboratory publications yet doesn't pat himself on the back, saying "My discovery will change the course of MS research." He also doesn't simply tell us what his discovery was—he takes us through his line of thinking (hunches) and tells us step by step what he did to make his breakthrough. He puts the emphasis on his curiosity. We learn a great deal from this kind of writing: The author is inventive and detail-oriented, does his due diligence on a topic, and is not full of himself—yet is justifiably proud. Well navigated!

A sample segment from an effective personal statement:

"...Although I cannot see a face when I remember Jessica, attached as she was to tubes and wires and machinery that breathed and pulsed for her, she is a presence in my life. I had returned to the 10th floor playroom for a spring performance. Every ambulatory child in the pediatric neurosurgery ward was present. There was anticipation of some temporal enjoyment, a little contagious enthusiasm, and a reminder of what's outside that ICU door. Grave illness leads quickly to feelings of abandonment, and although I was only seven, I could not bear the thought of these kids giving up on life and hope. Life holds too many possibilities. In the back of the room was Jessica, small and misshapen, contorted and motionless in her wheelchair and hooked up to more monitors than any patient I had seen. I began with something sweet and calming: Gluck's Melodie. I then tore off into the perpetual motion of The Carmen Fantasy. Suddenly a barrage of beepers and alarms went off in the back of the room. Two residents and a nurse pushed through the *other children, racing toward the sound. It was Jessica, and she had moved. How can I explain what that glorious moment meant to me? I continued playing as they wheeled her out with great rejoicing and excitement...I can't always remember their features or the color of their eyes, but I feel their presence—the children of the 10th floor: in every overture, in the first bow I take, in the last kiss to the balcony. They made me the young leader I have become and showed me that kids can move small mountains with big hearts. I owe them mine."*

Although this is only an excerpt of the full essay by a violin prodigy who is also a known humanitarian, we can still see the important and impressive essay writing qualities exhibited. There is no question that we hear emotionally and clearly about the phenomenal work done by this student. Earlier in the essay, he does not shy away from telling us that he is a professional concert artist who played Carnegie Hall and Lincoln Center at a young age, nor does he hide the fact that he single-handedly played hundreds of benefit concerts and hospital performances. However, look at the language he uses to pull us back from being overwhelmed or possibly put off by all of his achievements: "How can I explain what that glorious moment meant to me?" (a passionate and very moving expression) "They made me the young leader I have become and showed me that kids can move small mountains with big hearts. I owe them mine." (He thanks the children for molding who he is and what he has accomplished—showing that he is not a self-centered individual; then he graciously and symbolically gives his heart to them.) By the end of his essay, we not only get a full picture of all the attributes this student has to brag about, but we are left in a puddle of tears, because his essence, character, and deep commitment to his cause are all laid bare on the page. He is, throughout this essay, supremely likeable. Applicants do not realize just how important that likeability factor is for admissions officers.

You have now drilled down deeply to breathe life into your story—to find a characteristic or inspiration that reveals a small but significant part of you and to show the admissions office who you will be on campus. The essay may be finished, but the image you have presented is living on in the minds of your admissions officers as they determine their new class.

A word is dead
When it is said,
Some say.
I say it just begins
to live that day.
– Emily Dickinson

THE SHORT RESPONSES ARE TRICKY BUSINESS:

Some universities have short-answer questions that are very difficult to sculpt. The most important thing to learn is how to turn the question in your favor. No matter what weakness or bragging right the question asks for, you must spin it to bring out the qualities you want to project. Consider the examples below…

One university's short-answer prompt (25 words): Name one thing of which you are especially proud:

> *"I am proud of my commitment to humanism in medicine—having spent half my life working on health care equity for vulnerable children needing lifesaving surgery."*

Now, this could easily have come off as a short brag had the applicant not presented a redeeming characteristic. However, look at what this student did. She didn't talk about all the national awards she had won in biological/medical research or the papers she had presented at conferences. She knew that was all on her activity sheet and in her résumé. Instead, she dwelt on the "why" of her work. The "why" is what made her "especially proud." The "why" of her desire to pursue medicine was that she wanted to work toward equity in health care for vulnerable children. She kept the thread of her application even in a 25-word piece.

Another 25-word prompt: What do you wish you were better at being or doing?

> *"Chess—there's no upper bound to the skill level. As one learns more the bar keeps rising, and that appeals to my affinity for challenge."*

This is a smart answer for two reasons: firstly, and most importantly, this applicant truly enjoys chess; secondly, the answer tells a big story about the applicant. This student enjoys being challenged, enjoys rigorous thought, and doesn't take the easy way out—qualities important on an Ivy League campus.

Do not look at short-answer supplements and think that they will take very little time to complete. It is quite the opposite. Sir Winston Churchill said it well: "I'm going to make a long speech because I've not had the time to prepare a short one." Be sure that you allot plenty of time for your short responses.

Now, let's look at a very "real world" short response to a Syracuse University prompt: "If you had work experience, what skills and/or knowledge did you gain?"

> *"Through my work experience, I learned some valuable 'on the job' psychology about marketing a product: for example, nobody likes a slick salesperson. All customers want to feel that they are receiving both positive and negative comments about the item being considered for purchase; such objectivity leads to trust. An additional skill that I picked up is the application of a positive attitude. I found that if I started my day using positive visualization techniques (like imagining myself finding everything the customer wanted and making successful sales all day) I would, in fact, be more proactive in my customer dealings, and would end the day with more successful transactions. My two years of work in the field of sales have given me invaluable skills in communication— and good communication leads to a more open relationship between customer and business owner."*

Notice how this student pointed out very specific skills she learned and then explained not only how she used them on the job but how she could see using them toward future success in the retail business world. From a very normal kind of student work experience, this applicant demonstrated the value of having had a job and how she learned perhaps even more than she would have in a business class.

Finally, a note to international students about what *not* to do on the personal statement:

- For international students applying to American universities, don't make the core of your personal statement the fact that you have always wanted to study in the United States. The need for introspection and revealing something that is meaningful to you and has shaped you in some way is just as important for you as it is for an American student applying to universities in the United States.

- By all means, use local color and unique cultural experiences to reveal something compelling you have learned about yourself, but do not make your home country the theme of your essay. Think small and you will create an impact that is big. It's not a written piece about *where* you are; it's about *who* you are. You must stand at the center of your personal statement.

- To drill down further into the most successful college personal statement strategy, go to www.EssaySuite. com.

CHAPTER EIGHT

ACING YOUR INTERVIEW: **WOW** YOUR INTERVIEWER WITH THE LITTLE THINGS

M ost students feel as though the wild card of the admissions process is the interview, and it's easy to understand why. The prospect of being asked unpredictable questions by a stranger, while trying to come off as poised and informed, strikes terror into the hearts of even the most articulate candidates.

While you can't control who interviews you or what they're going to ask, you can still put yourself in the driver's seat by prepping. Practicing with an interview partner is one way to get more comfortable with the process. Be ready to discuss and expand on your areas of interest. For instance, if you say you have an interest in public policy or politics, you may be served questions about Facebook privacy issues, Israel vs. Palestine, Obamacare, prayer in the schools, to name a few. Be prepared with the latest news, or you're liable to wind up like Sarah.

Sarah, a classmate of one of my students, enjoyed her AP Government class and began to think that she would enjoy being a political science major in college. She talked about the possibility and even entered the major on her college application. The problem with Sarah's plan was that she never picked up a newspaper or watched the evening news, so she had no clue about current political events or foreign policy. Sarah didn't have time to read books involving political science—domestic and foreign security, comparative politics or international relations, and so on—because she was too busy taking six AP courses.

I am sure you see where this is leading. During Sarah's interview, right after the "So tell me something about yourself" question, the interviewer keyed into her major and began asking questions on topics like how the president could be better at Middle East relations, the place of the UN in international law, and which political theories of the past best define US politics in the present. All of this was intended to discover just how well informed and serious a student Sarah was in the field of political science. Floundering to come up with answers on the fly, Sarah made an impression on the interviewer—but not a good one.

Beyond simply knowing some substantive information about your planned major, it's also important not to forget about the "why"; why you're committed to that particular course of study and what draws you to it. Take Kevin's case: Kevin, the older brother of one of my students, applied to college as a pre-med major. He attended his interview, having never done science research during high school and having taken honors science courses but no APs. Truthfully, becoming a doctor is all he'd heard about from his parents while he was growing up. His father was a doctor, and his grandfather had been a doctor. Kevin hadn't actually done much personal investigation to find out whether or not he was right for medicine. When asked by the interviewer why he was considering medicine, Kevin could only say that, in his family, he grew up hearing that becoming a doctor would bring him respect and continue a family tradition. He hadn't done research on specific courses offered in the college's science departments, he knew nothing about internships on campus, he knew nothing about the type of science he wanted to study, and he had no plans for an externship or internship over the summer. The interviewer was not impressed. You need to know *why* you want to pursue the major you speak about in your interview.

Another student I heard about, we'll call him Terry, selected astrophysics as his major for college. He had never taken any science courses beyond biology in high school, but he was a science fiction fanatic. Based on all the sci-fi novels he had read, Terry thought astrophysics sounded…well…*cool.* When his interviewer asked him questions about physics and astronomy or about his "why" for choosing such a specific major, all Terry could do was cite passages that excited him from his favorite science fiction books. His responses, although passionate, demonstrated a lack of intellectual rigor in his course load and a total lack of investigation into something as important as an implied major at a college that prided itself on its science departments. A red flag had been raised in Admissions from an interview that should have simply been a nice, informative experience.

Whether it's astrophysics or classics, if you don't research the college offerings in your subjects of interest, you're in for a bumpy interview. Drew dreamed of attending an Ivy League school, and after visiting a few, he chose three of those universities as his reach schools. He selected his major areas of interest as the classics and English and was looking forward to talking with his interviewer about his enjoyment of the AP literature course he was taking as well as his hobby of reading the Greek classics in translation. Unfortunately, Drew forgot to review information on the classics and English departmental sites from his chosen schools. He didn't know any of the offered courses, the names of professors, or the research in which they were involved. As a result, when his interviewer asked him which courses he was looking forward to at the university and which professors he had heard of and wanted to study with, Drew had no idea. Awkward, and a red flag on an excellent student where there needn't have been one.

Another interview casualty I recently heard about that could have been avoided is the case of Matt. Matt was a nervous wreck about being accepted to a good college, so he decided to apply to twenty of them. As you can imagine, it's pretty tough to remember which college specializes in which programs and has which majors. So when Matt went to his interview for Princeton University, and the interviewer asked what his major area of study would be, Matt told him "financial economics."

"But," replied the interviewer, "we don't have that major. You can do a certificate in finance. Is that what you mean?"

"No," said Matt, "I remember being very excited about the financial economics major." As the interviewer began to jot down some notes (not positive ones), Matt suddenly realized that he had just discussed his academic excitement about Columbia University. What did Matt learn from this experience? (1) The Ivy League schools are *not* interchangeable, and (2) carefully research each college's offerings for majors, minors, and special classes in your field; and review your résumé before each interview.

Happily, Matt learned so much about Columbia University by the time that interview rolled around, he was telling the interviewer about programs and courses she didn't know existed!

The moral of these stories is that college interviews are not of earthshaking importance—normally. If you come prepared, know what your school offers in your areas of interest, visit the campus and/or speak to an administrator or professor, have a few insightful questions whose answers can't be easily found on the school website, and are able to look the interviewer in the eye (that is, you don't present with social anxiety), all should go smoothly!

How do you stay in control of the interview?

- *The usual first question is simply: Tell me about yourself.* This is harder than it sounds. If you handle this one correctly, you should be able to monopolize at least ten minutes of the interview describing the things you're passionate about. If there is one thing you have excelled at, like a business, an internship, an organization you founded, language fluency you possess, or a job you've held, speak in depth about it and provide examples.

- Keep moving from one interest or important résumé point to the next so that the interviewer has less of a chance to interject a question for which you haven't prepared. The key is to start with your greatest talent, intellectual curiosity, or biggest advantage. Is it a business or nonprofit you've started? Is it an artistic talent? Is it debate or school leadership? Is it your love of mathematics? Give as many examples and reasons as possible for why it's important for you to take part in this activity.

- The "why" behind what you do is what impresses. Explaining your *why* takes the interviewer into the core of who you are and who you'll be as a student on campus. It shows them how your presence there will improve and enliven the campus. The more you can tie your *why* into the reason you need the interviewer's alma mater to fulfill your higher education expectations, the more excited the interviewer will get about you.

If you can keep speaking about interesting things in your life and academic pursuits, you'll roll through some quality interview time without a sweat. Talk about winning a science fair, founding your business, or founding your nonprofit; winning a leadership award; taking a summer course in another country; backpacking and meeting students from all over the world and how that informed your views as a global citizen; pursuing an unusual art; returning to a grandparent's place of birth and how that affected you; working after school to make money to help your family while a parent is laid off; spearheading a community project. Analyze the reasons you were compelled to make these things happen.

BE FULLY ENGAGED

From the time you sit down, be engaged. Look the interviewer in the eye, extend your hand, and give a strong, friendly, professional handshake.

The interviewer will ask you to tell him something about yourself or will start with whatever the most special part of your résumé is. Yes, do bring your résumé. If the interviewer doesn't want to use it, then he won't, but usually interviewers are happy to have the document as a guide.

Do you have any other physical products to show your interviewer? A book you've written, a magazine you've edited, a short video of your company, nonprofit organization, or project? Anything visual is a bonus for the purposes of this interview. It will provide a jumping-off point for conversation.

An extra note here: Whereas in a job interview it's important to have more interactive conversations so that you can demonstrate your personality and penchant for teamwork, in a college interview save your questions for the end. This is the time for you to elaborate on your life's special triumphs and adventures, a time to show that you are as intelligent and articulate as your application is, and a time to show that you would be an asset to any campus and a great companion to any roommate.

LEAD WITH YOUR DEVOTION TO INTELLECTUAL VIGOR

Plan your segues from academic interest to academic interest and rehearse those segues until they are fluid. If you are discussing your interest in certain subjects, no interviewer is going to stop you in the middle. A thread of academic passion is just what colleges are looking for. Then, seamlessly plan a bridge into how you will demonstrate your love for those academic interests on campus.

For example, if you're a history major, perhaps you will become a member of the debate society or run for student government. If you play the flute and have an intellectual interest in music composition, you might talk about auditioning for the college orchestra and taking a beginning composition class. If you're a writer, make sure you have researched all the publications on campus so that you can discuss your favorites. Once you fully present that special piece of your résumé, say something like "Having accomplished xyz (a project, getting published, starting a business, concertizing) made me realize how important it would be to study X at this university." Then begin your monologue on the exciting courses in that area of study that you discovered by researching the university's departments and professors. Talk about the worth of each course to your planned academic concentration. Show that you have researched the work of a few professors and explain what excites you about their research and how you might love to become involved as an assistant in that research. Show your dedication to academic rigor and intellectual vigor. Students forget to do this during interviews, but it's important to remember that colleges will not accept you on your extracurricular prowess alone.

After you've presented the "intellectual you" to the interviewer, discuss the clubs, sports, and societies you hope to join. If you can come up with a way to communicate leadership or a new direction for one of those clubs, now would be the time to present that idea. Show the interviewer that you are a self-starter.

Finally, prepare at least three interesting questions about the school for your interviewer (however, if the answers can easily be found online, the interviewer will know that).

MAJOR ADMISSIONS FAILS:

- Parents insisting on sitting in on interviews with their kids.

- Students who walk into an interview without any prepared questions specific to that school.

- Students who wait until ten minutes before deadline to submit an application to a school they profess is their top choice.

- Students who spend their high school summers in camp, on teen tours, or home at the pool. (Better to spend them learning a new skill or interest that can inform future goals.)

- Students who put the wrong university name in their "why" essay. (Spotted on an essay for Tufts: "…and these are the reasons I know I belong at Duke.") Cutting and pasting essays from one application to another is a bad idea for so many reasons.

- Lying about having toured a college campus and then getting asked about the campus during an interview.

- Not cleaning up or deleting Facebook pages; the percentage of admissions officers that said they discovered things that adversely impacted an applicant's chances of admission is over 35 percent. Those discoveries can be something as simple as too many vulgarities on the page to alcohol consumption at a party. Privacy is dead, guys.

- Saying you want to attend X University because of its engineering program when it doesn't have an engineering program will get you a one-way ticket to the wastebasket.

- Faking your ethnicity so your application gets a second look.

- Thinking that your superpower standardized test-taking ability will make up for a B+ average in high school when applying to the Ivies.

- Listing more hours of extracurricular activities per week than there are hours in a week.

- Posting on Facebook that you're trying to decide whether to go to a private university or a state school because dad offered to buy you an M3 with the money he saves from State U.

IT'S THE LITTLE THINGS

If your interviewer buys coffee and asks if you'd like some, politely decline. All of your attention at all times must be on selling yourself—presenting your academics and special talents or experiences. If you're doing that right, your mouth will be moving too much to be drinking coffee. Besides, if you become animated and gesticulate enough to knock over your coffee cup, that's the memory your interviewer will have of you.

Guys, dress in a good sweater and slacks, or wear a jacket, button-down shirt, and slacks. No tie is necessary; but absolutely no ripped jeans. Girls, nice pants and a sweater or a sweater and skirt with tights and boots or pumps are good interview wear. Obviously you won't go to an interview in anything remotely revealing or inappropriate. You want to lead with your mind, not your cleavage.

Parents must never go with the student. Parents, if you're dropping off your son or daughter, be sure to do just that and assume you'll return to pick them up in an hour. You'll receive a text from your child when the interview is complete.

TYPICAL INTERVIEW QUESTIONS

- What is the most interesting class you took in high school?

- Which books have you read in the past year? Which was your favorite? Why? (Have some deep structure analysis ready to discuss on at least one book) Favorite authors?

- Why X College? What specifically is it about our extracurricular programs/professors/educational philosophy that interests you about this college?

- What are you planning on studying in college?

- Who would you spend time with if you could have a conversation with anyone? Why?

- What do you think is the biggest problem facing the nation? What insights can you lend?

- Why should X College choose you?

- What is your least favorite class?

- Tell me about a time you failed.

- Tell me about a time you showed leadership.

- What are your favorite extracurricular interests?

- How did you spend this past summer?

- What are your talents?

QUESTIONS INTERVIEWERS *SHOULDN'T* BE ASKING

- "Which AP courses have you taken?" or "What are your verbal and math scores?" Ridiculous, as an interviewer does not need to know this to craft his impression of you as a person and intellect.

- "What other schools did you apply to, and which one is your top choice?" While they're not supposed to ask this, it does come up. It's a sleazy question and requires a graceful but strategic response. Be sure to emphasize that X College (the one you're interviewing for at the moment) is at the top of your list. Then, offer two more schools on the same level or below—thereby demonstrating that in fact, their college is probably the first choice but that they may have a bit of competition.

DON'T FORGET TO INTERVIEW YOUR INTERVIEWER

- For an alumnus: What was your college experience like? What do you wish you could take advantage of today as a student at this college?

- How accessible are faculty members?

- Are there tutoring services available for the core subjects? Can a student sign up for them, or does he or she have to be recommended for extra help by a professor?

- Which courses of study are most popular on campus?

- Is the social scene driven by Greek life, college house parties, or mostly individual plans?

- How often do undergraduates get their first choice in housing?

CHAPTER NINE

POTHOLES, PITFALLS, AND HOW TO DODGE THEM

Beyond the obvious Big Mistakes—letting your GPA slip, choosing a less rigorous class over an AP, or letting your mom send the admissions office a box of home-baked cookies—students can make all kinds of poor choices that can impact their college futures. Let's talk about some of the more common ones.

DON'T SET YOUR HEART ON JUST ONE SCHOOL

Fixating on one school is kind of like falling in love with your first bike. You're jazzed by that bike. You think nothing will make you feel as proud as that bike. You name the bike "Jett," and Jett is the coolest. But when a bicycle specialist suggests you look at some other bikes, like "Stream" and "Blaze," you realize they have stunning and important features as well. The good news is that it's a nice problem to have.

It's the same with college: it's wonderful to have a dream school or even two, but if you narrow your focus exclusively to those one or two schools, you'll miss out on the fantastic research opportunities, proactive career services, strong alumni network, dedicated faculty, and nurturing environment of four or five other colleges that might be a perfect fit.

STOP LISTENING TO THE WRONG VOICES

Emily is a great daughter and friend. She works after school at Pete's Coffee so that she can pay for her own clothing and school lunches—a big help to her single mom who works full time as a paralegal.

Emily is first on her friends' call lists when they need advice about their love lives or parental conflicts. It's a tightknit group full of good kids, but all follow the least rigorous curriculum in school. Not Emily; she prides herself in taking all honors classes, forming close relationships with her teachers, and having a B+ average.

When it came time to apply to college, Emily's friends all decided to go to X Community College and pressed Emily aggressively to sign up with them.

"We'll all be together. The girls rockin' the world for two more years!"

"Why should we spend big bucks on college when we don't even know what we want to study yet?"

"Emily, everybody's doing community college now."

Emily was very conflicted. Just when she thought she had made up her mind to follow her friends, she had a discussion with Mom.

"Look, Emily," her mother began, "I've worked all my life so that you could have more. I don't know what 'more' means to you, but you're too bright and hardworking not to find out! You need a research university with lots of options and no worries that you'll have to apply all over again in two years. Go your own way."

This conversation gave Emily the strength to face her friends and explain that she was going to try something different. The girls wound up being proud of Emily as she was admitted to Boston University, majoring in business administration and management. Emily listened to her heart and reached for a future *she* determined, not one that was determined for her by the wrong voices.

DON'T FALL INTO THE GAP

A bright student—let's call her Zoe—studied hard in high school and had a nice A- GPA, but she felt lost. She wasn't sure what the point was in going to college, because she had no idea what to study—so she chose to take a gap year abroad and figure it all out. Now, a gap year can be a treasured and fulfilling experience, *if* you keep in touch with your college counselor in the interim so that you'll choose your gap activities wisely and know when application deadlines are for the following year's admission season.

You can probably tell where this is going. Zoe went to France for a year and took some classes that interested her. However, because the program wasn't part of a rigorous academic environment, she received no grades for the courses, and therefore, aside from having had a nice time abroad, had nothing to show for her gap year. Not only did she have no new intellectual progress to report on her résumé (which colleges look for, of course), she had no idea when applications were due for the following year.

Zoe arrived home in October, decided she wanted to apply early admissions to a number of schools, but then discovered she only had a couple of weeks in which to brainstorm and complete her Common Application, supplementary essays, and résumé. Zoe was a nervous wreck. Luckily she contacted us in time, and we worked together every day for two weeks to make her deadlines. Had she waited one more week, Zoe would have had to settle for being a freshman at the age of 21. Life has a way of slipping by when we don't think ahead. As things stood, Zoe's transcript was a hard sell to the colleges she *would* have been accepted to if she had presented grades and recommendations for her work abroad. The story ends happily, however, with a wonderful college match and a thrilled freshman—but the road to acceptance was hair-raising.

Moral of the story—make your choice an informed one by connecting with a qualified college admissions advisor *before* you decide on a gap year. A specialist can vet and advise you on the value of the program you're thinking of taking. And by keeping in touch through that year, we can ensure that your college dreams and plans stay on schedule. So stay true to your sense of adventure, but stay in touch!

BOOST YOUR RÉSUMÉ BY FOLLOWING YOUR PASSION

Regardless of the type of student you are, these are some extracurricular ideas that will get you noticed:

- Are you a film enthusiast? Start an indie film festival in your town.

- Are you a do-gooder with no particular expertise in social entrepreneurship but have a driver's license? Start an after-school car service for the elderly in your town to help them get to the supermarket or their doctors' appointments.

- Are you a musician who is not conservatory level but who would love to show colleges that you're serious about your avocation? Do an intellectual project on your favorite type of music: spend a couple of weeks in the summer studying that style with a master teacher, travel to the country of origin for the music you love best and do a musical documentary, learn Klezmer or Irish folk music, or write your own cadenzas to Mozart. Then write about that experience in a college essay, or do a research paper that summer on what you learned. Show your passion.

- Are you a writer? Write a column for free for your town paper. Or start a writer's center for vulnerable learners in your community and advertise it in the classifieds.

- Are you entrepreneurial? Start a business in the 9th grade and grow it. It doesn't matter what that business is, as long as you can trace its successes and failures in an essay. Perhaps you make enough to pay for a college course in something you always wanted to study; that shows an interest in the life of the mind and will pay off for you!

- Are you interestingly lopsided in your gifts? You might make it into an Ivy League school over a valedictorian who is only about grades.

ONLINE CAN BE OFF-PUTTING

If you're taking an extra academic course that is not part of your full, rigorous high school curriculum, colleges will look kindly on that because it shows that you were interested in learning something new and that you pushed yourself beyond what a typical high school makes available to you. By the same token, if your school doesn't offer a major AP course (like calculus, physics, or U.S. government) and you want to be competitive with other applicants in that field, you certainly can take the course online, and you will be viewed positively for the effort. But be aware that Admissions will judge your transcript based on the courses available at *your* high school. You will not be "punished" just because your high school doesn't offer as many APs as others.

However, if you decide to take one of your major courses online *instead* of in school, you had better have a very good reason for it. If you are a part-time conservatory or film student who attends an arts academy for half a day each day or you leave for an important lab internship each day and you take almost all of your AP or honors courses in school before you leave but don't have time for one or two classes, then admissions officers will understand some homeschooling or online schooling. After all, you are leaving school for other academic or intellectual pursuits.

If you simply decide that because you're a poor math student, you won't take calculus in school for fear that the calculus grade will pull down your average, then we have a different situation. Will you be filling that course slot with an elective? Will the other students in your class be taking calculus in school while you take art or business? If admissions officers see a trend toward lower grades in your math courses over the years and then see that you opt to take math online senior year even though it's offered in your school, that will absolutely raise a red flag. Be careful with your scheduling decisions and review them with a counselor each year.

Another red flag: if you are applying to a top-rung school, don't drop foreign language unless you are going to start a new one. Again, your grade thread in language will be under scrutiny, and your schedule will be judged against others applying to that college from your class.

DON'T PUT OFF TEST PREP FOR YOUR SATS

Don't dabble in standardized exams. Take three months to prepare for the SAT: do a section every night, and take a full exam every weekend (take an SAT prep course, if you can, to learn test strategy). By the time you sit for the test, you will be ready. If you don't receive the scores you think you're capable of, study for another month, and by all means take it again. But do something different before the exam this time. Take a review course, or get a little tutoring for trouble spots. Doing the same activity in the same way and expecting change is not working "smart." Try a new method of attack. After taking the exam twice and having done consistently smart studying and preparation, you'll have your representative score.

Don't bother taking the exam a third time. Your GPA and transcript rigor are *king* for colleges. Your standardized test scores should simply fall within the college's range. If they do, it won't be the test that gets you in or keeps you out. Not that a 2400 will hurt anybody—that's awesome!—but that can't be all you have to show. Colleges will be searching for your quirky, jagged edge. What will make you an interesting addition to the campus and classroom? That's where you need to put your effort (aside from excelling in your high school coursework) during these test-intensive years.

I do advise, however, taking two subject tests, whether or not you think you'll be applying to schools that require them. If you are a strong student in a particular subject (holding a B+ to A average), take a month to study for the subject tests—get a couple of review books and read all the sections. Study the material (much of it should be review for you by now if you're taking the tests immediately after taking the courses in school), answer the review questions, and take all the tests in the books. Take the June exam if you see that you can score above 700 (for a top-tier or Ivy school) or the equivalent of what you imagine might be the best score needed for the colleges on your list. The reason for this is that if you're applying to Ivy or top-rung schools, you need two subject tests anyway. If you're applying to other good schools or state schools, remember that these colleges and universities are also receiving applications from students who are using them as their safety schools, should those students not get into their reach or target college choices. Those students have strong portfolios with all the standardized tests a college might desire—including subject tests. If you want to be considered a strong candidate among those types of applications, show a little hustle and desire to demonstrate your academic breadth by taking subject tests. The tests will strengthen the impression your class grade provides. One thing standardized exams can do is equalize the playing field. If you're a strong student in language, you're not going to get a 500 on your foreign language subject test. Admissions officers use these tests to see whether the student's high school inflates grades or if the student's grades are true reflections of his or her intelligence.

If you would like to receive a list of recommended, carefully vetted online resources and prep companies, visit this link: www.AdmissionMarketplace.com.

WORK IT! Studies have shown that 30 minutes of exercise before taking a practice test can significantly enhance your test performance. Exercise boosts the blood (hence, oxygen) supply to the brain. Just check the studies by researchers at Boston University School of Medicine to learn more (but do it while jogging!). Get on the treadmill or go for a run before practicing your standardized test sections.

DON'T SKIP OUT ON THE TOUR

The campus tour is the secret sauce. It's the final ingredient—the chief factor that informs your thrilling choice for the next four years. Take advantage of the opportunity to visit as many campuses as possible. The results, I promise, will be unexpected and meaningful.

I always suggest visits to the top four or five schools a senior is interested in. These are some of the most significant trips that you and your family will ever take. Colleges know how difficult it is to schedule a number of tours during the hectic school year, and that's why most of them have sign-in books of some sort. Admissions understands that if you're taking the trouble to visit the campus, you are truly interested; and although never scientifically proven in an article entitled "What Percentage of Students Who Visit Campus and Are Academically Competitive for That School Actually Get Accepted Over Those Who Don't Visit and Are Equally Competitive?" I can tell you that for the top schools in the nation, a visit counts. Don't think that in our Big Data society, admissions offices will miss the fact that you say their school is your #1, yet you haven't demonstrated that kind of interest by a visit.

More importantly, your college tour gives you the chance to experience the "campus gut reaction." More times than not, a student has two or three favorite colleges in mind, then walks onto campus at one of them, feels the butterflies in the stomach, and exclaims: "This is it! This is my school!" This reaction is golden. Firstly, it gives you an academic target at which to aim your energies and dreams; secondly, and equally importantly, it clarifies for you what you *don't* want in a school, because you have finally seen what you *do* want. For these reasons alone, it's worth visiting your top choice campuses.

Remember, attending an information session, taking a campus tour, and schmoozing with students online at the coffee shop or in the halls of your future department of choice are the best ways to get a rounded profile of the college during your visit. Once you are accepted, most colleges have Accepted Student Overnights during which you can make a final assessment. Go to those. You're finally the one being courted—enjoy it and determine which campus gets to have *you*.

WHAT YOU DO *AFTER* YOUR TOUR MATTERS, TOO!

Once you've made your visit, taken the tour, attended an information session, and inquired about interviewing at that school, you need to follow up quickly with an enthusiastic email to the regional officer or director. This email should be sent out the day after your visit, if possible, especially if you asked questions or introduced yourself to an admissions officer or tour guide. Writing the next day will remind them about you and the interest you showed.

In a nutshell, what you want to accomplish with your follow-up note is to convey excitement about the school and distinguish yourself by expressing a particular interest or important fact learned through the campus visit. Tell Admissions what valuable news you learned from the info session: Is there a new science lab being built, a new emphasis on computer science, an entrepreneurial major recently instated, a sporting event added, or a professor you met who took the time to talk with you about his latest book? The more specific you can be about what propels you to that college, the more of an imprint you'll make on the mind of your admissions officer.

Now, if an administrator or professor does take the time to meet with you or give you a tour of a campus facility, send a handwritten thank-you note. The impact will be special. Most students never think about writing a few meaningful lines and putting them in the mail. Again, you'll want to be as specific as possible when you thank the person for the talk, the time, or the tour. If you discussed the possibility of freshman research internships, be sure to mention that. It will remind the professor or administrator who you are. This is all about developing a relationship.

If you had a particularly good campus tour, get the name of the student who led it. This is a great excuse to write an email to Admissions and let them know you're interested; you're proactive (because you got the tour guide's name); and that your etiquette is first class (you're thanking Admissions for a great session and tour, and complimenting their choice in guides). Tell Admissions exactly what you liked about the tour. The more specific your email, the bigger the impression you'll make.

DON'T FORGET TO INVESTIGATE
COMPETITIONS AND SCHOLARSHIPS

Scholarships exist in every field you can imagine. Do not wait until the end of junior year to begin your search (although there are plenty of important scholarships that you can apply for through senior year). These competitions include essays and can take a good deal of time to get into shape. Ideally, you'll want a couple of consulting sessions with an admissions counselor to learn how to craft winning essays specifically for these competitions. Many require a certain strategic approach that you wouldn't know without a little help. Some of these national scholarships provide enough funding to pay for half a year of college or more, so they are definitely worth the effort!

SHOW LOVE OF LEARNING FOR LEARNING'S SAKE

Proving love of and zeal for learning is more important than being president of Key Club or newspaper editor-in-chief…if you can show it in an interesting way. Yes, it is essential to have a strong GPA in the most rigorous courses offered by your high school. And yes, even your high school's rigor is judged by colleges: your guidance counselor sends in a high school profile with each application (describing the curriculum, the grading or ranking system, the philosophy about AP courses, the range of students in the graduating class, and so on). However, taking 11 APs and doing well does not necessarily show zeal for learning. It might, but more often it shows that you are academically competitive and have a strong intellect. What shows zeal for and love of learning for learning's sake is what you do outside of school when you don't *have* to be learning. Over the summers, have you taken advantage of college courses in other countries or at home? Have you studied fields to which you wouldn't normally be exposed during high school? Are you a reader? What literature do you read in your spare time or on vacations? Some college applications will ask you that.

If you're a scientist, do you participate in research programs after school or during the summer? Are you aware of programs like MIT's Research Science Institute (RSI), the Rockefeller University Summer Science Research Program for New York State residents, the High School Summer Science Research Program (HSSSRP), the High School Honors Science/Mathematics/Engineering Program (HSHSP), or Boston University's Research Internship in Science and Engineering (RISE), to name a few?

If you plan on writing a paper (upon culmination of your summer research at one of these programs) and submitting that paper to a science fair, ask each program director before applying whether that particular summer program encourages and assists its interns with the outlining and editing of a disciplined science fair paper and if that research is even allowed to be taken off campus for presentation by the student at national and international science fairs. These are crucial points to know before starting a summer program.

If you're an engineer or entrepreneur, have you tried to develop technology that will help deal with niche problems? Have you practiced your business skills in a start-up company? Consider developing an app or a prototype for something that will help a community deal with a small but identifiable problem. Participate in start-up businesses that could use some of your expertise in coding, communication/social media, or copywriting.

If you're a computer science student, do you study new languages over the summer to bolster your knowledge and effectiveness? If you're a theater student, do you study voice on the weekend in a conservatory program or study Shakespeare in London during the summer to further educate yourself and to work on dialect?

If you love foreign language, do you study different languages in the summer at programs like the Middlebury-Monterey Language Academy? Have you checked into scholarships for such programs? They exist.

Could you tutor students during the school year to pass on your love of a particular subject?

Are you the kind of self-starter who will hunt for competitions and grants in your fields of interest? Admissions likes to see that you are a mover who has sought out funding for a new social action or business opportunity. Those opportunities will expose you to learning on a higher level.

Again, you can see how a little advance planning and careful consideration can make a big difference in where you're accepted to college and what you learn about yourself as a leader for life. The more you're on top of things, the less overwhelming the college admissions process will feel. The saying "Knowledge is Power" was never more true than it is in the pursuit of self-discovery or admission to the best-fit school.

In the next chapter, I'll reveal a few things you probably *don't* know about the Ivies, Stanford, and MIT.

Here's a hint: *Assuming that all Ivies are created equal is a fatal mistake.* I promise you that the "eenie-meenie-miney-moe" method of choosing the right Ivy reach schools is not a winning technique.

CHAPTER TEN

INSIDE THE IVIES;
YOU KNOW YOU WANT TO KNOW!

I often talk with students who nurture Ivy League dreams but who don't understand that the Ivies are in fact very different from one another. You can be a top-tier student and still not be a good fit at the particular Ivy you've selected. Just like people, universities have distinct personalities and vibes. Knowing what each school is about will help you avoid spinning your wheels by applying to a school that may not ultimately be the right fit for your personality and goals. In this chapter, I'll take you on a mini-tour of these august institutions and give you a behind-the-scenes glimpse of their special characteristics.

One thing that Ivy and top-tier schools do have in common is that they want to be loved for who they are. Knowing their specific personalities will help you differentiate them in your essays and other application materials.

Harvard: No other university has a brand like Harvard's. The school is renowned throughout the world. For students who attend, however, there are some very real critiques and points you should be aware of as interested high school seniors.

Harvard's approach to information sessions and undergraduate education in general is a bit stiff and off-putting; that should initially tell you something. Not only will you have to be among the brightest students in the nation to make it on this campus, you'll also have to be among the most independent. No one holds your hand or goes out of their way to find you or mentor you here. You'll need to create your own quirkiness and color on campus and fight for leadership positions. And fight you will, because achieving leadership on Harvard's campus is a highly competitive endeavor. It obviously can be accomplished but not by the timid.

Harvard's students are typically very focused on their preprofessional careers from the time they arrive. They tend to be hypercompetitive and arrange their extracurricular activities accordingly. You don't come to Harvard specifically for the arts—although you may be brimming with those kinds of talents, and although there are plenty of creative people at Harvard. You come to connect, to prove to yourself that you've got what it takes emotionally and intellectually to make it at the top in this hypercompetitive world. That proof, of course, is not a bad thing with which to exit college!

It's still true that the hardest thing about Harvard is just getting in, as the school is notoriously liberal about awarding course As compared to, let's say, Princeton, which is a hard-core intellectual environment with a grading system to match (although, at this printing, Princeton has determined to remove grade deflation).

However, Harvard has been trying to promote more of a fun-loving image with its hilarious pranks against Yale (for example, running fake campus tours at Yale and telling all the high school visitors to apply to Harvard instead) and holding some very creative award ceremonies. In the "No, I'm not kidding" category, Harvard holds a spoof science Nobel Prize ceremony in which, for example, U.S. and Indian scientists recently won a prize in the field of medicine by finding a way to stop uncontrollable nosebleeds with cured pork. So Harvard does have its fun side, but make no mistake about it, the students here are focused, assertive, and very competitive.

There are no special formulas to ensure acceptance at Harvard. In fact, the university's admissions policy is often considered to appear rather whimsical to many students. However, if you're within the top five in your high school class with exceptional standardized test scores and the most rigorous AP/IB curriculum to match, *plus* you have an outstanding passion, advocacy, talent, or entrepreneurial project that has been developed during your high school career (so that you show a thread of passion)…you'll have a shot.

Princeton: Always looking for the best scholars, lately Princeton is especially hunting for entrepreneurs and engineers. This bastion of intellectual rigor and honor (the honor system is a point of pride among students and faculty alike) already has a worldwide reputation for being the place where rigorous intellectual scholarship flourishes and is nurtured via mentoring by a close-knit, accessible faculty. You won't likely find a completely self-involved professor at the helm of your class at Princeton, because amid the rigor of social sciences, humanities, mathematics, science, and engineering at Princeton beats the heart of a liberal arts school—the sort about which films are created. Professors are there to teach undergraduates. As one of my students recently expressed, "Dr. B, I'm in love with learning again."

The university is now however, also a bubbling, innovative hub of engineering and entrepreneurship, as much for engineering and finance students as for marketing and creative types.

The best tip for a Princeton hopeful is that, along with top scores and GPA, you must be a strong, analytical writer. Princeton looks extra carefully at your writing classes, recommendations from English teachers, and your essays—with good reason. You'll even be writing papers in mathematics classes at Princeton!

Princeton has big school spirit for its athletics (and especially for games with Harvard), alumni affiliation that cannot be beat as far as outreach for internships and post graduation jobs are concerned, and a proactive career center. They want their "Tigers" to succeed in and beyond the classroom.

Stanford: Although not a member of the Ivy League, Stanford is certainly respected to the same degree. SU has become one of the most sought-after college tickets in the world. Students see Stanford as the mecca of computer science/tech, design, and engineering, as well as business innovation. Now that Stanford has locked down that innovation vibe, although continuing to look for the most brilliant STEM and entrepreneurial students with that "Palo Alto" focus, the university now puts special effort into attracting the type of students who would normally attend Princeton or Yale—creative types and intellects in the humanities, social sciences, and arts. The school is presently trying to expand its name from being the place to go for tech/engineering/computer science/entrepreneurship to a university that has equal renown in the arts and humanities as well.

University of Pennsylvania: An exceptional real-world kind of Ivy League experience, at Penn, you get the feel of the intellectual "tower" while you're in classes, but outside, your extracurricular life is brimming with activity, the opportunity for every type of internship, entrepreneurial centers like Pennovation for projects, funding for products and start-ups, and business and pre-law coursework through Wharton. All of this is tough to match on an undergraduate level. Let's not forget that Penn is one of the few universities with the distinction of having among the greatest number of billionaire alumni (a club that also includes Princeton, Harvard, Yale, Stanford, Cornell, and USC).

Penn has vibrant school spirit and the athletic and social life to match. The university looks for legacies with top numbers (highest scores and GPAs matter here), but Admissions must see an excellent fit between student and school; otherwise, legacy will not lead to acceptance.

Pay careful attention to your supplementary essays for Penn. Also, research Penn's outstanding interdisciplinary undergraduate programs: the Huntsman Program in international studies and business, the Jerome Fisher Program in management and technology, and the Vagelos Scholars Program in the molecular life sciences. These are some of the best interdisciplinary degrees out there. One of my students said it best, "Not only am I studying with the authors who wrote the texts for class, but each class at Penn is a real-world laboratory. If I could take seven courses each semester, I would." Penn loves its early admission candidates.

Dartmouth: A tucked-away Ivy outpost that loves its scholar/ athletes, and a powerhouse academic environment (which is also strongly geared toward the Greek system), Dartmouth is well aware that it is a little insular, so the college divides its calendar into the most creative arrangement you'll find in the Ivies. To give students time to intern, study abroad, start a business, or just explore a new field, the school's "D-term" affords unusual freedom and flexibility. Dartmouth allows you to customize your own academic calendar via four 10-week terms per year (fall, winter, spring, and summer); you are allowed to enroll in any 12 terms during your college education (with some restrictions). For the students who want real-world work experience during their college academic experience, Dartmouth offers fascinating options.

Rising juniors all stay for the summer following their sophomore year and take a full course load. However, they can use an entire year for "leave-term learning," during which time they can take an internship, do public service, or conduct field research. Many Dartmouth programs even fund students for leave-term opportunities.

Dartmouth students can also take their education abroad, choosing from an extensive list of language and topical study programs around the world. The four major paths for off-campus study are Dartmouth Language Study Abroad, Dartmouth Foreign Study Programs, Dartmouth Exchange Programs, and transfer credit from another four-year degree-granting school.

Columbia: The legendary Core program maintains a love and appreciation for the liberal arts among Columbia students. Freshmen bond over the Core and talk about the value of such shared academic experiences for everyone from language majors to history majors to engineers. Columbia also has a nice policy of "no class Fridays" so that students can engage in one of Manhattan's many interesting internship opportunities. The city of New York is the campus and canvas for Columbia students, as they experience a peerless artistic and cultural scene, along with an exciting array of quirky and diverse restaurants and clubs. There's something for every budget—even the college student's.

Columbia is not for everyone—there is not a lot of handholding or close professor/student relationships. The administration at Columbia is also notorious for not being very involved in the undergraduate experience. Undergraduates have to be independent types who go out of their way to create a network and mentorships, but there's a vibrant extracurricular scene on campus, with everything from comedy to music to social action, as well as ethnocentric clubs. The in-class education and preparation for professional life or graduate studies is, without question, excellent.

MIT: Though not an official member of the Ivy League, MIT is of equal renown. Its stunning STEM curriculum and hardcore work requirements are not for the weak of heart. The MIT student must have the right personality and study ethic, aside from exceptional math, science, and technical prowess. The course work is brutal, the students attending are brilliant in their STEM capabilities, and pulling a high GPA at MIT is about as tough as it gets. This is one of the reasons that pre-meds who know they will absolutely go into medicine are less likely to choose MIT, a school where students with extraordinary math and science aptitude (who might go on for PhDs or who are naturals in engineering) make up the majority. In order to ease the freshman transition into courses that have very tough exams, MIT instituted a policy for first-semester freshmen known as "pass, no record": If students don't pass the class, there's no record of having ever taken it. In the second semester, the policy switches to "ABC, no record."

You have to enter MIT understanding what you're in for; you may never feel like the top of the class again. However, without realizing the STEM brilliance out there, you would have no great mountains to climb or hurdles to jump in order to push yourself to be the most innovative and clever you can be. Understand that MIT wants you to succeed and that your rewards upon graduation will most likely be great.

Cornell: Cornell is doing everything right, right now. Students in all majors can take entrepreneurship classes. The programs in architecture, hotel administration, industrial & labor relations, engineering, and computer science are tops. While it is a STEM and entrepreneurial heaven, it is very tough in those fields, with a fierce level of competition that is not for the faint of heart. However, students love the campus and programs and are thrilled by the high quality of internships they are afforded as undergraduates. Cornell loves to be loved, so if you are truly interested in attending, apply early decision.

Yale: You haven't heard of "Boola Boola" for nothing. The campus brims with huge school spirit every day and bursts with it during *The Game* weekend (i.e. the game between Yale and Harvard—one of the oldest and most famous college football rivalries). Every student is an intellect *and* a leader *and* fascinating in some way. There is a Yale type: If you're an innovative engineer who rides a unicycle, a published science researcher who does ballroom dancing, a concert instrumentalist who does stand-up, a nationally recognized debater who sings bass in a jazz a cappella group, a writer who speaks five languages and has a record album, or a brilliant theatrical talent who writes and directs for DRAMAT and also majors in computer science…you'll pretty much feel at home here. I kid, but you get the idea. The SAT 800 students are present and accounted for at Yale, but the special, very unusually talented are more the rule than the exception.

One point I should add: Recently, Yale has been rolling out the red carpet for the best engineering/STEM students they can find. Although the university is working to strengthen its computer science program, they're determined to keep their fair share of STEM stars.

One of my rising seniors at Yale explained, "If you're not already an artist and innovator when you enter Yale, you'll at least catch the bug during your four years. No one leaves untouched by the culture of leadership and creativity on this campus."

Brown University: The smart, free-spirited, quirky member of the league, Brown is extremely selective and not just in relation to GPA, standardized test scores, and leadership, but in spirit. Brown only takes students whose spirits would soar in its dynamic, outspoken, interdisciplinary college environment. To get the most out of Brown, you have to be willing to experiment academically and be comfortable with a very interdisciplinary, as opposed to pre-professional, environment. Brown's Program in Liberal Medical Education (PLME) for pre-med majors is excellent and turns out some of the more relaxed and happy medical students in the nation because of the vibe on campus. No one will be holding your feet to the fire to get you to major in a "sensible" subject at Brown. You can certainly have a brilliant and engaging college career as a pre-med or economics major at Brown, but the intellectual engine on campus that will surround you will be made up of double majors in renaissance studies and political science, science and technology studies and archaeology, environmental studies and Egyptology…you get the idea. Brown's website explains: "At Brown ...we challenge you to develop your own core. Our open curriculum ensures you great freedom in directing the course of your education, but it also expects you to remain open to people, ideas, and experiences that may be entirely new."

A FINAL WORD ABOUT THE IVY LEAGUE: SOUR IVY GRAPES

There are many ways to get a fine education in our nation; liberal arts colleges like Reed, Kenyon, St. John's (Santa Fe or Maryland locations), Bowdoin, Middlebury, or Vassar are tough to beat for individual attention and smaller scholarly classroom experiences with close mentorship.

However, because of recent backlash against the selectivity of our Ivy League institutions, along with Stanford and MIT, many students are being led to believe that they cannot get this type of supportive mentoring and deeply meaningful, life-altering learning from these schools as well. Students are being overwhelmed by media suggesting that the singular reason for going to college is getting a job afterward (as if colleges can *assure* you of a job upon graduation these days)— citing statistics that Ivy and top-tier graduates do not do better financially than graduates of other colleges; that the alumni network among Ivy graduates, for example, doesn't seem to provide jobs in a preferential fashion; and that students could have a much easier time in high school without taking all the tougher, challenging courses required for possible admittance into the Ivies (yes, we'd all have an easier time in life if we didn't have to deal with challenge and competition, but that's not reality, guys). These articles and talking heads suggest that students who attend Ivies would do just fine attending any of our nation's colleges, since it's the student, not the school that makes the future happen. Furthermore, why not skip the process and do a Thiel Fellowship (if you are among the entrepreneurially brilliant and also very lucky), go to coding or vocational school (if the traditional academic route is not for you), or travel the world and figure out your path later? It could be a fun and fulfilling option but not for everyone. And there we have it…the Ivy League is *also* not for everyone, but for those young scholars who seek the nourishment of small seminars for their lively literary or political debate; who love the process of critical analysis and empathic growth; who bend toward studying a lyrical piece of writing or an elegant equation as readily as someone else is thrilled by conquering Ruby on Rails; who thrive on competing, intellectual sparring, and learning beyond the expected or accepted. This kind of student also has to choose his or her new academic and social home with great care, because not every school will fit.

It might be true that if you are a proactive, professionally hungry student, you will do well in the job market regardless of where you have gone to college. It's still important, though, to think about who your circle of friends might be at school. Who will be your influencers? Will there be students to push you toward your personal best? If you have spent your high school years challenging yourself intellectually, artistically, entrepreneurially, etc., then why wouldn't you try for the most rigorous and esteemed universities in the nation—the top tier and the Ivies? Admittance is not a sure thing. Everyone knows that; but you can't get admitted if you don't apply. And you may not apply if you don't understand what a gift that four-year experience can be—academically and financially (because the scholarships are need-based and generous). It is an opportunity to be surrounded by professors of once-in-a-lifetime stature and spark. It is a social connection to an unnervingly brilliant and talented pool of friends, advocates, and adversaries—all equally important characters in life, who will push you to be your best or better than your best. The Ivies and schools of that ilk still present you with uncommon academic and creative riches along with valuable social capital: There will be coffee with your politics professor debating Hobbes and Locke, dinner with your English professor dishing up Dante's *Inferno*, elegant equations to turn on their sides with your engineering professor, and business plans to concoct with the director of entrepreneurship. The Ivies and top tier open doors for summer internships through alumni connection and name recognition. I am not saying that those of you who are in the top ten percent of your high school class will not find academic challenge and success at schools of all tiers; rather, I am saying that some students will find, in the Ivies and top tier, exactly what they've been dreaming about all though their rigorous high school adventures. Do not let the wrong voices embarrass you for wanting to reach if your academic or artistic talents make the reach worthwhile. Students are not cookie cutter—neither should they expect their college experiences to be.

Do not listen to naysayers who might have sour grapes about not having gained acceptance to one of these schools, or who might be pushing certain social or business agendas, or who might be well-intentioned but ill-informed young people hitching a ride on the popular threads of social media. Please, if you have the desire for this kind of education, extend yourself and try for it. These four years never come again. You *will* be accepted somewhere wonderful if you've achieved academically and have made interesting attempts to explore your authentic self in high school. The first step is admitting that's what you want.

CHAPTER ELEVEN

HIGH SCHOOL; YOUR FOUR-YEAR TIMETABLE: WHAT YOU NEED TO DO AND WHEN

High school is important for so many reasons, the greatest of which is that this is when you embark upon a meaningful and qualitative period of self-discovery. Find what you love to learn. Embrace even those courses you don't love—because they are life experiences. Work as hard as you can to determine your path to college. If you're reading this book as a freshman, good for you! If your high school career is already underway, don't be tempted to skip through the sections here that are aimed at underclassmen; it's just possible that you might have missed a step in preparing for your college admissions journey, and you need to be aware of that.

I see the admissions journey as being as much a smart marketing endeavor for life as it is an academic endeavor. Finding *you* requires more than putting in the necessary hours to ace your subjects or joining after-school activities because your friends have joined. It requires a thoughtful, unexpected adventure that you take as early as possible and in as many fields as are interesting to you to determine where your light will shine in high school.

Remember that the college application bins in admissions offices are crowded places. It takes something beyond your grades to stand out: it takes having made that special journey. Even if taking that journey doesn't lead you to admission at the school you want, you've still discovered glorious things about yourself that you wouldn't have by sitting in after-school clubs or hanging out at parties every weekend. Take the time you need to find your extraordinary tilt during high school and shine!

Look at your college application as an important painting. First you will apply broad brushstrokes, by setting out a strategy for success beginning in freshman year—through scheduling the right courses and activities and exploring leadership opportunities inside and outside of school. By sophomore year your head should be seriously into your studies, and your after-school hours should be used to explore a specific leadership position, talent, or business opportunity that you can turn the crank on in a big way. Begin to learn what you're made of. By junior year, you're ready to fill in the details: standardized exams, higher development of your talents, and founding or furthering your community project, organization, public service, business, or political advocacy. If you're a STEM student, begin research at a lab or with a mentor, write a research paper, and position yourself for local or national competition. All of this will prepare you for an exciting and busy senior year of writing your college applications and demonstrating to yourself and Admissions that you are a dynamic person and a go-getter—someone who will be interesting in life and on campus.

FRESHMAN YEAR

Choose the most rigorous courses offered at your school, but leave time for one fun elective to give your day a breather. There has to be one class in your schedule where your grade is not based on two hours of homework and studying each night.

Schedule a meeting with your guidance counselor so that you can get to know each other. Be sure to talk about your strengths, weaknesses, and talents, along with special programs that exist through the high school or in connection with the high school. For example, some high schools have connections with city or neighborhood fine and performing arts schools. Are you the kind of student who must have an arts curriculum in order to flourish? See if you can arrange your course load so that you can leave school earlier each day to attend afternoon programs or classes at a conservatory or arts school. Perhaps your high school will give you credit for those classes on your transcript. Are you an athlete who is going for a county, state, or national title? Perhaps you need to finish early each day to practice with your tennis teacher or a coach. You get the idea. Freshman year is the time to talk about all of your options. Most students fall into the trap of a standard curriculum when, in fact, they may not be standard students.

Give yourself the *option* of taking an SAT subject test this year if you have mastered the subject with a strong grade. Of course, most subject tests are taken after a student has completed the AP curriculum in that subject (because they have just been through the most rigorous training and will certainly succeed on the test if they have succeeded in the class); however, if you have consistently scored at the top of your honors course in biology, chemistry, and so on, then you have an excellent chance of scoring in the 700s on your subject tests. Go for it. The fewer standardized exams you have to worry about during sophomore or junior year, the better.

By January of freshman year, you should be investigating the summer programs that sound fascinating to you. Contact a college advisor for vetted and highly recommended programs that best fit your fields of interest.

SOPHOMORE YEAR

If you're not developing your own extraordinary tilt, get on it. You're only in high school once! Explore!

Finding one's authentic self can take a lifetime for some and is certainly rare to come up with in a one-year period, so if you are reading this advice early in your high school career, please, please act on it. Why leave the discovering and developing of your talents and leadership skills until junior year or senior year first semester? Think about the stress! Junior year needs to be used for broadening your intellect, enhancing your talents, doing something expansive with your exceptional tilt, and, of course, studying for your standardized exams! You'll need to keep your GPA high because colleges scrutinize junior year grades closely. Although you can develop yourself and make some extraordinary leadership happen during junior year, remember that a bulk of your time will be spent studying for AP courses and preparing for and taking standardized exams. And senior year has its own demands and challenges. You're much better off taking the initiative now, right after you finish this book!

THINGS TO KEEP IN MIND THIS YEAR

Your grades are under a microscope now. Work your hardest to do well. This is the year when most schools allow students to begin taking honors and AP courses. If you think you'll be applying to top-rung colleges and Ivies, strive to achieve As. Hopefully, your freshman year grades gave you a good start. Although top schools do like to see an upward trend in grades, make no mistake about it— they are used to seeing grades in the A range from freshman through senior year. That doesn't mean a couple of Bs along the way will keep you out. It just means in that case, you will have to achieve more *outside* the boundaries of school (extracurricular leadership, a special academic project, competitive victories through one's talents, public service, etc.) to be competitive in that group.

Let me say a word about AP or IB courses at this point. I understand that the rigor of these courses and the stress placed upon the end-of-year standardized exams have gotten a bad rap recently. Yes, they will be tougher classes than your honors courses. Yes, you will have a hectic, stressful couple of months before exams. And yes, you have the freedom to choose not to take AP or IB courses. However, I hope you step up to the challenge. Look, AP and IB courses play a bigger role in your life than just showing Admissions your discipline and intellectual spunk. They also broaden your knowledge base, teach you how to think and write critically in ways you have never before experienced, give you an idea of what college classes might be like (although, regardless of what you've heard about the difficulty of AP classes or IB programs, they are in no way as difficult as top college classes in similar subjects), and show you what you're made of. If you are afraid to take the intellectual plunge in high school, how much more frightening might freshman year of college be for you?

Part of life is learning how to balance the tough stuff, deal with stress, fail, pick yourself up, and then figure out how to succeed. Taking a challenging academic course of study in high school—whatever that may mean for your particular academic engine—is a wonderful beginning to understanding what it means to rise to the challenges in life. There, I've said it: AP and IB courses are good for your intellectual and emotional growth.

THE DIFFERENCE BETWEEN AP AND IB

There are 34 possible AP courses (taught at a level *approximating* an introductory college course's difficulty), with associated exams administered during the month of May. The highest score one can achieve is a 5, and with that score usually comes college credits and/or the ability to skip introductory courses in college. Students can pick and choose which AP courses to take and therefore can demonstrate their academic strengths by taking APs in their strongest fields. Taking more than seven or eight APs by end of senior year does not increase one's chances of getting into a top-tier or Ivy League university but certainly might increase one's interest and in-depth understanding of a subject area. AP courses allow for a great deal of flexibility regarding when a student can take both the course and the corresponding exam. Many students now self-study certain APs online (like music theory and computer science) and take the exams online. The curriculum includes a great deal of material to digest and memorize, along with training in textual analysis. AP students may be given a choice of whether or not to take the AP exams in May–so there is still the option of taking an extra AP course just for the joy of learning, without the necessity and bother of an extra exam. Some high schools, however, have made it mandatory for students who take the class to take the corresponding exams by denying AP class credit for those who do not sit for the exam.

IB classes teach students to be critical thinkers and writers. With its inquiry-based approach, IB courses take a global and interdisciplinary look at topics (an approach common on college campuses). Students can choose to take individual IB courses or a full IB diploma–a program that runs for both junior and senior year and requires college-level classes in six academic subject areas. The six course fields are mathematics, English language and literature, foreign language, a natural science, a social science, and a course in the arts or a second class in one of the aforementioned core courses.

One of the major achievements of full IB diploma students (and one that prepares them well for college) is the writing of a 4,000-word paper on an academic topic of interest. The project is undertaken with the mentorship and guidance of a faculty person.

Carolyn M. Callahan, chair of the Department of Leadership, Foundations, and Policy at the University of Virginia, explains, "The content of AP science and math courses often does not enable gifted students to achieve an in-depth understanding of the discipline...There is limited opportunity for the pursuit of individual interests or passions in these courses. The IB program provides greater opportunity for in-depth pursuit of a topic." The takeaway is that a student cannot go wrong with experiencing either program.

Take the practice PSAT given in the fall. The score does not count, but it will give you a good idea about where you stand and what needs improvement in your math and critical reading skills. Then you can begin working on those areas.

Begin using your vacation time to check out colleges online. See which might have the environment that's best for you. You might already know that you want a "rah-rah" school, a big university, or a small liberal arts college. Students often have a pretty clear idea about what sort of school appeals to them by sophomore year. However, do not close yourself off to other possibilities, because your interests may very well change over the next year or so and so will your decision on the best college environment. Visit websites like Unigo (www.unigo. com) to read comments by students about their universities and YOUniversityTV (www.youniversitytv.com) to enjoy online tours of your college choices.

By December, start researching good summer programs in your fields of interest. Perhaps you want to audition for a well-known summer music/conservatory program, intern at a tech firm or law office, take an immersion course in an unusual language or one you already study, take an academic program abroad in courses not available at your high school, or do science research in a renowned program in the United States. All of these are wonderful ideas, but there are so many more options.

Sign up for SAT subject tests in the spring: Be sure to put your June test dates on your calendar early and base your study schedule around them. Begin study for these exams at least one month prior to the test date, and work nightly through each section of your review books. I recommend Princeton Review Books for this endeavor, but if you really want to put yourself through an intensive and more challenging study effort, use the Barron's Review Books in addition. When you score well on those practice exams, you're ready for anything!

JUNIOR YEAR

Junior year is not for the faint of heart, that's true. It is a year replete with standardized testing, the stress of balancing your rigorous course load, leadership positions in full swing, plus visits to colleges. It's enough to drive any student to Starbucks! But resist the caffeine or this could be you!

You Should Switch to Decaf If:

- You've been on Wikipedia for 23 hours and still can't figure out why there was no Pope Sixtus VI in your AP Euro textbook.

- You've been studying calculus so long that the voices in your head have bodies.

- You're writing code to circumvent the character limit on the Common App.

- You've spent more than 45 minutes trying to figure out the difference between Chicago and Turabian citations.

- The idea of applying to 15 colleges suddenly sounds good to you.

- You've found Waldo.

- You're cursing out the Common App for not having an 11th line for your expertise in miniature golf.

- Your English teacher assigns a ten-page paper, and you ask if it's okay if you're ten pages over.

- Your study break to Starbucks results in your request for something larger than a *trenta*.

- Your guidance counselor sees you in the hall, asks how you're doing, and your response is "Not now, I'm busy!"

- Your regional admissions officer has received 12 emails from you asking if he's gotten the previous 15.

Junior year is the year to keep your eye on the prize. Put every hour you can into your GPA but not to the exclusion of elevating your leadership profile *outside* of school. Continue the thread of leadership or talent that has brought you success so far; or create a novel leadership project or position that relates directly to the thread of interest you have followed until this year. Be careful about résumé padding—if you've never cared about joining the debate team, now would not be the time to start.

Begin your PSAT studying by August and continue through to the exam date in October. It may seem unimportant to qualify as at least a commended student on the PSAT, but it does have its perks. Being a National Merit semifinalist makes colleges sit up and take notice. It says a number of things about you, not the least of which is that you either have excellent natural intelligence or were focused enough to prepare in advance to succeed on this test. Either way, it's a win. Being commended is also something very noteworthy to achieve.

Start your search for scholarships and grants. Look for grants that are available through public service organizations, write for them, and begin a creative community outreach project, if you haven't already developed a defining leadership activity outside of school. If you have a thread of service since freshman or sophomore year, now is the time to bring your work to some sort of climactic stage—whether it's organizing a major fundraiser, major media exposure, or winning a competition and networking with that competition's board to move your project to the next step. This is the year to make things happen in your leadership sector.

Are you concerned about being in a field like biology, which highly regards science and engineering fair victories, while you haven't won any to date? Here's an example of the kind of thing you can do to turn the tables in your favor during junior year: become founder of an archival journal of all research abstracts and papers from your high school, and hold fundraisers to fund its annual publication. Volunteer to create an online source for your high school science fair abstracts, so that freshmen and sophomores can see the type of work that has been sent to national fairs. Interview the heads of research at all neighboring high schools to get the secrets of a winning project, and offer the interviews in an online product to STEM students. Now you have an entrepreneurial project that reaches through the application and says, *Look at me!* This is a way to turn weakness into advantage. Colleges may be more impressed with your entrepreneurial attitude than they are with another person from your class who won a few awards.

Schedule a meeting in the spring with your parents and guidance counselor to discuss college options. Before the meeting, create an outline of the 15 schools you are most interested in. Also have a heart-to-heart discussion with your parents about finances. Is the college choice dependent upon scholarships?

Organize your SAT, ACT, subject test, and AP exam dates. This bears repeating: remember that even if your chosen colleges do not include a request for the subject test, take two anyway. This shows a college that you are a hard worker, motivated, and a self-starter—all qualities needed on campus.

TAKE YOUR PSAT/NMSQT IN OCTOBER.

Feel free to visit some colleges on weekends in November or early December of senior year. You do not need to see classes as much as you need to feel the campus atmosphere and speak to students. In the spring of senior year you will spend a few overnights at your top choice colleges—preview weekends—and that will allow you time to sit in on classes before making your ultimate choice.

Now listen—regardless of how many friends are taking their spring breaks to visit colleges, you should plan to stay home and study for your AP exams. They come up "fast and furious" after spring break, and you'll need all the time you can get to feel like a master of your material and to keep your stress levels down.

Remember, if you are Division I or II caliber in athletics, be sure to discuss options with your coach regarding NCAA requirements for eligibility.

The Final Stretch:

- Ask your two favorite teachers for recommendations by June. Hand them your résumé and highlight any parts that you think will be valuable for them to know. Even your favorite teachers may not know that you intern at a law office during every vacation or that you run a business outside of school or that you write a political blog.

- When it comes time to create your senior schedule, make sure it's the most rigorous one you can handle, within the most rigorous course load offered at your school. If you are hoping for a top-rung or Ivy League college, you must take AP-level English, math (preferably Calculus AB, unless you are an engineering major, in which case you would be expected to take Calculus BC), foreign language, history, and science. Now, in some cases, if your résumé shows that you're a completely humanities or social science person, you may get away with taking AP Statistics in school, if you are worried about what your grade would look like in an AP Calculus class. However, I would strongly advise taking the AP Calculus as a homeschooled or online *additional* math course so that Admissions can see you still met the challenge of the calculus course. Why should you do this? Because, although many top universities won't admit it, they have concerns about students who seem to take the easy way out of difficult courses. For some schools, not having AP Calculus is actually a showstopper. Therefore, why not study it in a stress-free environment? You can use this to an advantage by explaining that, although you know you will have greater likelihood of using statistics in your career than calculus, you decided to study statistics in school; however, because you wanted to be sure to expose yourself to calculus and experience the most rigorous curriculum, you also took calculus as a homeschooled course of study. This way, at least your colleges see that you have a reason for your choices and that you care enough to go for the challenge as well.

- If there is a fine research paper that you have completed in any discipline, make sure to keep it on file. Then send it either as a PDF or hard copy to the department head in the university to which you're applying.

Summer of junior year is for having experiences that can mold you and help you to grow in new ways. This could mean taking a job; traveling for new academic experiences; finishing a creative project you started in the fall—a novel, a film, an art or photography portfolio; doing science research in a university program; working on an article for publication with your research mentor; or having an adventure of a lifetime that somehow ties in with your high school thread of academic, business, research, performing arts, or social entrepreneurial passion.

Be sure to complete your Common Application. Your personal statement, an extracurricular essay (always wise to have), and the standardized sections of the Common Application should be finished by mid-August. You'll be so thankful to have all that done once you see how many supplementary essays there are to conquer. If you can have your top three to five applications plus supplements completed by the time you begin school in September, you will be giving yourself the best chance to excel in your senior year courses. Way to go!

WAIT! What if by junior year you're not where you thought you'd be? Don't melt down!

There's always time to improve and smart ways to do it. This is the year you'll be bearing down on academics (standardized tests, AP courses, keeping grades high). Is standardized test taking a problem for you? Perhaps the issue is about your time management skills. What do you do when you need to change the way you habitually deal with demands like time management? You create a new standardized test study habit! Aristotle was on to something when he noted, "We are what we repeatedly do. Excellence, then, is not an act but a habit."

You create a habit by doing the same thing at the same time every day for a month. Let's find a way to make sure you do the important things you have to do every day so that you improve your math or reading scores without getting distracted by unimportant "noise" during junior year. The best way to reach your goals is to make the study process habitual. But be patient. It takes 30 days to create a new habit.

New Habit Action Plan: Choose a new habit you'd like to create:

- Doing one page of the Common App every day; writing a new essay draft every three days; allotting the time every day to choose video and photos for a high school video highlights reel: Visit www.ResuMotiv.com for help with this.

Write down:

- What you're going to wear when you do this task (maybe you like doing college application work in your pajamas or sweats)

- How you're going to get ready for it

- Set a time to do the task, ideally early in the day, and put it on your calendar. Maybe you need a cup of coffee and a cookie…and who doesn't?

- Stick to this routine for thirty consecutive days, and it will become your new, improved habit.

Don't check email or voicemail before you do your new habit every day. You must disconnect. If you practice the techniques I'm teaching you, you will learn how to conquer those standardized tests. Patience and organization are half the battle. Don't *ever* walk into an SAT or ACT without having studied and prepared in an organized, *daily* fashion for at least a month.

Do what it takes to get it done:

- Perhaps you need to find out which are the best practice review books and problem sets for you. Different students react differently to the various review books—some like the challenge of the often frustrating and difficult Barron's Review Books; others think the Princeton Review is more on target. Perhaps there's a review class that has its own materials and specialists who can guide you through them. Know yourself and your work style and choose wisely.

- Perhaps you need to find a tutor in the subject that causes you the deepest pain. A two-month intensive tutoring schedule can bring your score up 100 points if you do your tutor's practice assignments and take at least one full, timed practice test a week (on the weekend) in quiet testing conditions away from the active rooms in the house.

- A tutor can also explain to you whether you're overthinking the questions, taking too long on each answer, or not reading the question in front of you (but reading what you think it's asking). You'd be surprised how many students initially just don't read exactly what the question is asking, especially if they're moving too quickly.

- Focused, intensive studying is worth the effort. Keep your eyes on the prize: If you're worried about your social life going out the window, try to remember that only a finite amount of time will be going into your preparation. It's worth a few months of sacrifice and keeping that laser-like focus to actually win the prize—a healthy and challenging academic fit for college and a socially exciting home for the next four years. Once you take the test and succeed, your social life will still be waiting for you where you left it.

So Many Tests, So Little Time.
How Do I Choose between the SAT and ACT?

I know, I know–students can just go nuts trying to decide which of these two notorious standardized exams will best demonstrate their natural intelligence and analytical ability. Please know that the SAT is being changed...*again*...in 2016. Let's break it all down:

- THE SAT format, for those of you taking it in the spring of 2015, has three sections: mathematics, critical reasoning, and writing. The ACT has five: mathematics, English, science, reading, and an optional writing section. Students may believe that they can finesse their way out of doing a written piece if they take the ACT. The problem is that many colleges and universities will require their applicants to complete the writing section, so students may need to take that optional part anyway. Of course, if English and writing are your strong suits, then the SAT may still be the best option for you.

- The SAT focuses on a student's aptitude in verbal and reasoning skills. Students who can more easily wrap their heads around more analytical questions tend to do well on the SAT. The ACT is, by design, a test of achievement and information learned over the course of high school. Because the ACT is more material- and achievement oriented, many students feel more comfortable taking the exam. But be aware, if you have a weak background in science (for example, if you are not comfortable with data interpretation), the ACT may not be the right choice. Now, counselors will say that only a basic knowledge of science and the ability to make inferences are required. In fact, for the most part that is true. There are three basic question types: data interpretation, research summaries, and conflicting viewpoints. The official ACT website insists that *"Advanced knowledge in these subjects is* **not required,** *but background knowledge acquired in general, introductory science courses is needed…" So if you have had little exposure to the sciences and are not terribly concerned about the SAT critical reasoning questions, opt for the SAT first.*

- *For those who are comfortable with mathematics tests, either the SAT or ACT will work for you. The ACT actually tests the same math as the SAT but also includes trigonometry and plane geometry.*

- *For those who have a rich and broad vocabulary, the SAT might be an excellent choice.*

- *Students always ask which exam has more difficult questions. The answer is, it really depends on how you test. That's why, before you decide on which exam to take, you should spend some time with practice sections from review books on each. You'll know after a few days of studying which test comes more naturally to you. What you might want to know more about is the arrangement of difficult questions on each exam. The answer to that is more cut and dried. The SAT questions become increasingly difficult as one moves through each section. The ACT questions are totally random in their order of difficulty.*

- *Some students prefer one test over the other based on the way the test deals with wrong answers. On the 2015 SAT, students are penalized for incorrect responses. On the ACT, students are not penalized if they guess incorrectly, and the score rests on the number of correct responses only.*

- *The College Board will be releasing the* **NEW** *SAT in spring 2016. The test will include three sections: evidence-based reading and writing, math, and an optional essay. Students will no longer be able to simply* choose answers–they'll need to justify their answers. The new score scale will revert to 1600, with a separate score for the essay. Test takers will not be penalized for choosing incorrect answers. The new reading and writing section will ask students to cite evidence for their answer choices, and reading passages will range from science, to history, to literature. Obscure vocabulary will be eliminated for more widely used collegiate vocabulary like *synthesis* and *empirical*. The math section will no longer allow calculators for all portions. Areas of the math section will focus on data analysis and real-world problem-solving, algebra, advanced math, and additional math concepts. The essay will be an optional component, though highly recommended.

- Will this test be the golden child of standardized exams? Who knows? But it's coming, and you have to prepare. *So try out practice questions for both exams, either online or in a review book, and be on the lookout for practice questions from the new SAT. See which best allows you to show your skills. Good luck!*

TEST ANXIETY

- Perhaps you have standardized test anxiety. Take a class that puts you in the test-taking situation at least once a week. After sitting with a room full of students taking a multi-hour SAT or ACT once a week for a couple of months, as well as spending that time learning how to think for the exam, you will see your scores improve dramatically.

- Another possibility for you is to look into colleges that do not require the standardized SAT or ACT: Did you know that these schools exist? NYU, for example, will take your SAT/ACT score, or three subject test scores (which are much more class-material based), or three AP exam scores. There are so many others: Muhlenberg College, Bard, Bates, Bennington, Bowdoin, Franklin & Marshall, Hobart & William Smith, Hampshire, Middlebury, Mt. Holyoke, Pitzer in California, University of Arizona, Wake Forest, WPI, and more.

By junior year, it's important to have leadership in at least two activities, one or both of which can be outside of school. But what if you've gotten a late start? Are you a junior with great grades but no uncommon flag (that is, something special you have accomplished that gets you noticed by Admissions)? Although you won't be able to show a long thread of dedication to a cause, subject, idea, or talent, remember that young people discover interests and callings unexpectedly. If this happens to you in junior year, then you'll still be able to write about how it happened and why you are pulled to that activity.

Play catch-up and begin to identify yourself with a major activity now. Your activity should take place outside of school, since leadership positions are unlikely to be handed out to new participants who are juniors already. It can involve nonprofit/outreach, business, sciences, government, or arts (if you're involved in the arts); or it can include two or three out of the batch.

The moral of the story is, luck doesn't find *you*—*you* have to make your own luck. Do it outside the school walls, where there are no politics or popularity games to prevent you from succeeding. And study, study, study for the best grades possible in your classes. Yes, junior grades are every bit as important as you've heard.

SENIOR YEAR

This is one of the most exciting years of your life! Take many deep breaths and try to appreciate every minute. You will want to remember this year.

To-do list for September:

- Meet with your guidance counselor to check over your first few college supplement essays and the Common Application personal statement. Discuss any shifts that have occurred in your decisions to apply to certain universities—including which schools, if any, you have chosen for early admission. Discuss the wisdom of applying early for your specific set of circumstances: your grades, your finances, your scores, the pool of students from your high school against whom you'll be judged, and so on. Make sure that you have two safety schools and at least three target schools on your list, in addition to a few reach schools. These days, it's wise to apply to ten schools if your GPA and scores put you on a competitive level for college admission. Be a focused multitasker as you continue with your leadership roles inside or outside of school. Stay on target with all important dates and deadlines on your calendar.

- Remind your two teachers about recommendations. Teachers get overwhelmed, and it's an important gesture to gently remind them about sending your recommendations out on time.

- Division I or II athletics folks: ALERT! Make sure to file the NCAA eligibility forms.

Seniors, Clean Up Your Facebook Act...Now!

Seniors, we understand that your sense of privacy is, shall we say, flexible, but admissions officers have flexibility, too. They can check your fluid high school privacy on Facebook and Google at their discretion—without warning to you and with possibly devastating outcomes.

According to a Kaplan survey of college admissions officers, more than one in four respondents admits to checking Google and Facebook for information on applicants. Of those officers who conducted a search, 35 percent uncovered information that negatively affected an applicant's chance of admission. This year, the online search about applicants has become even more vigorous.

Some scholarship sponsors have started requiring applicants to accept Facebook friend requests as part of the review process. In certain cases, your own alumni interviewer may find you on Twitter and follow you. There are many ways to access a student's "truth" these days. To avoid the discovery of such truth, many seniors have wiped their Facebook pages, deleted their accounts, or even set up fake accounts under other names. Some go so far as to set up "do-gooder" accounts with only listings of wonderful community service on it—for example: "Today I helped out at the City Center Book Drive," or "Today I spoke in front of a middle school group about bullying." You get the idea. Well, so does the admissions office. They are wise to those who say they have no Facebook page; many officers will check under your name or variants of your name for a social media online presence, and you had better hope they only find one of which you're proud.

In CNN's opinion piece on Facebook's role in college scrutiny, Debra Shaver, the dean of admissions at Smith College, had this to say of student writing on the Internet: "I do think that students can be held accountable. Those of us at residential colleges are building communities; I want students in my community who behave in a way that is civil and respectful and thoughtful."

William Fitzsimmons, Harvard's dean of admissions, admits that, although not a practice, admissions officers "…may have occasion to encounter an applicant's digital footprint. This often can be positive for applicants to the degree that it helps demonstrate their range of interests and accomplishments but could be negative if it raises serious questions about character or judgment." Hmmm… "may have occasion to encounter," huh? Sounds like you might want to take this seriously.

In an ideal world, colleges would commit to a modus operandi regarding their use of Facebook and social media spying, but as of yet, there is no consensus on use. Better to be safe than sorry, my precollege friend. Tell your friends in advance not to tag you in party photos, block any friends who use crude language on your site, or, better yet, just leave Facebook during senior year. Even the best students can get caught in a photo in an apparently compromising scenario where they are only bystanders. You spend so much time perfecting your résumé, activities list, and applications—why would you not perfect your online social presence?

To-do list for October:

- Complete last-minute details on your early applications: whether ED, EA, or REA.

- Submit rolling admission applications. Be sure to have all of your necessary scores and your transcript ready. All sections of the application must be submitted before a decision can be sent to you.

- One more "go" at the SAT: If you absolutely have to take another SAT, be sure to do it now. You will still have time for your scores to reach your early college choice. I rarely recommend a student take the SAT during senior year, but if you have put in a great deal of effort studying and preparing over the summer, then you certainly deserve another chance at your best score.

- If there are unusual circumstances to your schooling: (for example, homeschooled, part time at a conservatory or film school, or online schooling), send a note to your admissions officer at each college and thoroughly explain your situation. You can also put this explanation in the education section of your appended résumé. It will be read.

To-do list for November:

- Your early applications should be submitted. Hopefully you have most of your college supplements completed by now if you put in the work over the summer, and you can begin work on your final essays.

- Those pesky FAFSA forms: Remind your parents to please complete the FAFSA forms online at www.fafsa.ed.gov for your financial aid.

- Request supplementary recommendations: Early November is a great time to ask an extra teacher, your boss, or internship director to please write a supplementary recommendation on your behalf to your early school and your top three schools. The trick is to ask someone who can write about you in a way that presents a side of you, whether academic or professional, that the admissions office may not have already seen. Such a letter will be welcomed by most colleges and universities. They understand the importance of multiple perspectives on a student, and they know that if a third teacher is going to take the time during a busy fall to offer praise and a new frame of reference about this student, the student must be a worthwhile investment. You may have recommendations from two different departments, like English and history, but you want to underscore the fact that you are a dedicated and well-trained writer. One way to highlight this is to have your third recommendation also come from an English teacher (honors or AP). There is nothing wrong with building up an arsenal of proof about a particular talent.

- The LAST-CHANCE SAT...if you absolutely insist. You already know how I feel about taking a last-minute SAT, but if you *must*, you can take it in November. (Hopefully it's not your third time. That doesn't usually move the needle much.)

Midway into November, send an email to your regional admissions officer to show demonstrated interest (if you do not know who that officer is, ask your guidance counselor). This note should also act as an update on any new or continuing activities from the time that you submitted the application. If you have won any awards, started a new project, or simply want to tell Admissions that X University remains your first choice and that you will attend if accepted, write those things in this note. You can find templates for admissions officer emails in the Template section of AdmissionMap™ at College Admission Central. Visit: http://collegeadmissioncentral.com/products-services/

To-do list for December:

This month marks your final push through application supplements. Stay on top of your calendar, and you will have all of your materials in on time and without stress. Try to complete remaining forms and essays as early in the month as possible, so that you can enjoy and revel in your December break!

- Proofread: Do a final proofreading of all essays before sending them out into cyberspace. You'd be surprised how many rejections happen just because of a few typos.

- *Don't* wait till 11:55 pm to submit by deadline! Server crashes happen frequently. That would be a devastating finale after all your hard work.

- Make this month count with your grades: Colleges take the first semester high school grades very seriously. These grades not only show that you are a finisher but that you continue to care about doing well. Colleges are looking to embrace that kind of student.

- If you have updates to your application, send an email to the admissions officer at each school where you've applied.

- If you've been admitted through early decision, hurray! Be sure to notify the remaining schools you've applied to so that they can extend admission offers to other deserving students. If you have been admitted through early action (EA) or restricted early action (REA) and would still like to keep your options open and hear from other reach schools on your list, please contact the safeties and at least open up those spots to other seniors.

To-do list for January

Happy New Year!

- Keep your grades up, whether or not you have been accepted early. If you have not received an acceptance, it's just a bump in the road. Maybe you will consider yourself lucky that your early school didn't accept you, because a reach school from your regular decision (RD) applications might come through in April! It happens all the time. So keep the faith and keep your grades up. A serious downturn in grades can sink you.

- Keep your college interviews organized on your calendar.

- Still need to do campus visits? Make them now.

To-do list for February:

- Send updates and a demonstrated interest email to your top choice school.

- Study hard in school, keep your leadership activities, special projects, or internship/job an important part of your life, and have a great winter break!

- If you have updates to your RD application, send them this month, along with a message to your top school that promises attendance if admitted. Believe it or not, that's actually important when admissions officers are deciding among students. When they hear you will absolutely attend, it can help decide things in your favor. Every school wants to be loved.

March Madness!

The wait seems interminable! This is the toughest month for seniors because it's too early to start studying for AP exams, it's post winter break, and it's time to start the official countdown to April 1st.

- **Take this time to review updates on the college websites of your choice**, keep up your GPA (colleges do send out warnings and rescind notices when course grades that were formerly in the A range suddenly drop to B and below), and dream about March 27th–April 1st!

April: And the lucky college is…

Here it is! The year of hard work, worrying, and waiting has reached its exciting climax and you have some very nice college choices! Congratulations!

- Attend overnights and acceptance weekends. Enjoy, but behave responsibly. Colleges will find out if you acted in ways unbecoming a pre-frosh.

- While on campus, talk to as many students as possible. Listen to what they say about campus culture, courses and professors, career services, study abroad programs, and any of the clubs that you might like to get involved in. Do the students love their school? Is there pride? Can you see yourself both giving and receiving from this university? You will know for sure which school is in your future by the time these weekends are over.

- Sit with your parents to assess the financial aid offers from each school. Be proactive. If you are deciding between two colleges—one that offers more aid versus the one you really want to attend that offers less—ask your parents to call the preferred school's financial aid office. See if there is any leeway in the offer. Sometimes, students are pleasantly surprised.

- Be sure to submit your decision by May 1.

- If there is a waitlist in your future, then send a note that says you would like to remain on the school's waitlist. Meet with your guidance counselor to see if they can place a call to the university on your behalf or at least find out your chances of being accepted from that list.

Are there other recommendations, award notifications, or materials you can send to the committee that might move things in your favor? Connect with your counselor in June to ensure that your final transcript has been sent.

- But...*please* do not count on a waitlist. Make your decision. Be proud and happy about it, and move on. If a call comes from the waitlist, great. If not, you won't miss it anyway.

- Most importantly, enjoy the fact that you are now in college and the world awaits your special gifts! You have done so well!

- Congratulations! Have a cup of coffee!

CHAPTER TWELVE

SEVEN WAYS ADMISSIONS HAS CHANGED IN THE PAST YEAR; WHAT YOU DON'T KNOW *Can* HURT YOU

1) **FAFSA foolery**: This FAFSA hint will blow you away. Did you ever think about the order in which you list your FAFSA schools on the application? If not, you'd better start thinking about it. If you want to be seriously considered for your target or top safety schools, mix up the order in which you list them on FAFSA or list them alphabetically. It has been intimated by admissions officers that if your first few schools are all Ivies and you put something like Vanderbilt in the middle, Vanderbilt might take notice and defer or reject you. That's just the way the new game is played. Big Data tells a college that the conversion rate for applicants

is highest for those students who place that particular college in their top three choices on FAFSA. Makes sense, in a subliminal messaging sort of way.

2) **Big Data is watching you:** In the foreseeable future, you must know how to handle Big Data. Every note you send, call you make, query through online sources, or posting on Facebook can and very well may be mined and collected for information by your colleges of choice. Be judicious in how you get in touch with your college admissions officers and where you post your college interest. If you post on Facebook that you're excited about visiting Duke, and someone from Admissions at your safety school, Tulane, is trolling the Facebook sites of its interested applicants and sees your post… bye-bye, safety school. You get the idea.

3) **The demonstrated interest game**: If you visit a college and you're not given a way to sign in to let Admissions know you were there, your job is to go home and write an email to your regional admissions officer or to the general admissions office and let them know you were on campus and loved it! More than ever, demonstrated interest is playing a part in acceptance. If a college information event is scheduled within driving distance of your hometown, make sure to sign up and attend. This information is all collected, and Admissions will take notice.

Part of attending one of these events is coming prepared with a question for the admissions representative. If you're very patient, you are likely to get a minute to ask that question in person after the program. It's worth waiting in line behind a crowd of other students for the opportunity to interact one-on-one. Make your question specific, and remember to mention it in the quick, polite email that you'll write to that representative the next day. Thank the officer for coming and sharing information about X University, and mention that you enjoyed speaking to him or her and having your question answered. This serves as a reminder to your regional officer of your interest in the college.

Also, if a college you're interested in sends you a communication through email and asks you to check out programs by clicking a link...click the link! If you intend to apply with the objective of possibly attending if accepted, this is a small way of showing demonstrated interest in our Big Data world.

4) **Your campus visit can be the deciding factor that gets you accepted...if you know what you're doing.** As noted in an earlier chapter, if someone takes the time to sit down with you or give you a tour of a campus, sit down the next day and handwrite them a gracious thank-you note. Find the name of the student who led your tour and mention it in your email to Admissions. The more specific your email, the bigger the impression you'll make.

A final tip about campus visiting—if you have to choose which colleges to visit first, you might start with those farthest away from you. The reason? Colleges pay extra attention when students from outside their geographic region visit. It's a specially noted example of demonstrated interest.

5) **The lifejacket for the B student:** Did you know that there's a way to get college admissions to notice you that has nothing to do with your grades? As long as you have a solid GPA and average test scores, you can win at college admissions! You have to go out into your community and **do something helpful and creative** for that community with heart and a little sweat equity. If you can create such a project, you will be admitted over the student whose parents spent all kinds of money on their summer service trips. Be authentic and give back.

6) *When* **you submit is more important than you thought:** Take note about when you click "Submit" on your applications. Colleges have now determined that, aside from ED or EA applicants, the students who apply early in the year for regular decision (in October and November) are the ones who are most interested in attending those universities. This flies in the face of the old idea that admissions officers don't pay attention to RD applications until after deadline. Now, however, they are looking at the month that RD applications were submitted and are giving a little extra consideration to those students who have gotten it

together to submit a well-developed application early in senior year.

7) **Merit scholarships are used for more than just determining merit:** In the new admission cycle, applying for your college's merit scholarships is now considered a demonstration of interest. It takes a good deal of time to write the extra essays usually required for such merit awards. It's perceived by the college that if you apply for their merit awards and receive one, such a measurable scholarship could sway you from your top choice school. Don't take this strategy lightly. Spend the hours to do the supplementary award essays and apply. This is a way for universities to attract students who are looking for excellent alternatives to their first few choices, and for generous funding to help with college debt. This is a new way to show colleges that you are serious about them and that you might accept them if they accept you.

BONUS: WARNING...

Admissions officers of the current cycle are sick of reading self-impressed essays. It doesn't matter how much you've accomplished if you can't write about it humbly. If you don't sound likeable in your personal statement and supplementary essays, you'll be staring at the rejection pile.

CHAPTER THIRTEEN

WHAT YOU SHOULD BE DOING IN THE SUMMER BEFORE COLLEGE

What I'm about to tell you comes from having interviewed over 250 students of recent high school graduating classes—and all have made the same points: They never feel totally prepared to take on college because the weaknesses that a college career exposes are the very skills you needed to fix while you were in high school—but didn't have time. I'm talking about working and socializing on a whole new level.

The summer before freshman year is extremely valuable—if you compartmentalize it and use it in the right way. Of course, some of those summer hours might be needed for your job, travel, organizing, and shopping for the upcoming, most exciting time of your life. But, as engaged members of this self-taught, online course–savvy generation, all of you can learn college lifesaving skills by spending a couple of hours a day in the summer practicing these key areas of expertise: research writing, computer skills, time management, networking skills, and public speaking.

Research Writing Skills: You'll want to set up some after-school sessions with your English teacher in June; lobby for a research paper crash course in your school when exams are over—you just want to know the essentials and any tips your teacher can provide on structure, citations, and figuring out your voice for the assignment— that is, are you summarizing, persuading, analyzing, responding, or observing? Each of these would give a different purpose and voice to your writing. If you can't arrange some time for extra help with your English teacher, meet with a college student for a session or two during the summer on the most important things to know about writing and formatting a research paper.

Computer Skills: Learn Microsoft Office Suite, if you haven't already. It is critical for college work, as well as for internships during college. Become familiar and competent with Word, PowerPoint, and Excel at the minimum. Online tutorials can get you started, but hands-on practice is essential.

Time Management: Managing your senior year schedule and staying on top of your grades should have given you a leg up in this department. But if you thought it was a hefty task to maintain your academic and social schedule during high school, just wait until every fascinating club, lecture, party, theatrical performance, political debate, athletic event, coffee meet-up, professor's office hours, and career services meeting is offered over the same few days during college. You will need to come up with a calendar system that works for you so that homework and daily study don't suffer.

Set alarms on your phone or computer calendar for waking up in the morning, waking up after a study nap, and for classes (always figure in the number of necessary minutes to get to and from class). Have alarms set a day before a test and a week before a major paper is due. When you set a meeting, put it right into your phone calendar to sync to your computer.

Print out your weekly calendar and tack it up in your room—just because it's a good idea to have backup. Occasionally, our electronics fail us. Put all assignments on your calendar the day you get them. Don't wait. Waiting is the enemy of good grades in college. If you leave assignments to the last minute, you'll most likely pull grades below your ability level—unless you're very lucky or very smart! Tackle the most difficult projects early in the day so that you don't feel overwhelmed in the evening.

Set a couple of hours every single day that are Facebook/phone/email/Twitter/Instagram FREE times. Just go dark and do your work. You will feel refreshed, and there will be much more to see when you return.

During exam week, set two alarms for yourself if you're going to take a power nap: one alarm on your phone and the other on your alarm clock. It's very unsettling to fall asleep with your calculus in the middle of the afternoon and then wake up at 7 p.m. and know that you still have eight hours of work ahead of you.

Networking Skills: To know how to network involves practice. You'll need to practice a 30-second elevator pitch that can lead into a one-minute expanded story. Additionally, practice the hand-eye coordination of looking someone in the eye, stretching out your hand, smiling, and saying nice to meet you—all at the same time!

Think about the number of times you'll need to use these skills…at college acceptance receptions; all during the first month of college at mealtime, meetings with advisors, RAs, housemasters, and career service representatives; and in early winter for internship recruiting season (you should expect to have two, possibly three, interviews before internship decisions are made—so that's a lot of communication/networking skill needed to nab that first job). This is the beginning of understanding that you will always be selling yourself—professionally and socially. Now is the time to learn how to do this elegantly and adeptly.

Public Speaking: Public speaking is not something that is on every senior's mind, but getting some informal practice in crafting a short talk and speaking in front of an audience will be of tremendous value to you for college and in your professional life to come. Research the location of the nearest chapter of Toastmasters, which you can find online at www.toastmasters.org. Toastmasters is a friendly educational organization that coaches public speaking and leadership skills at locations throughout the United States. Determine the best club for you based on your schedule. This is not a huge time commitment—one or two hours a week—but it is an activity that will change your life.

CREATE A PROFESSIONAL AND EFFECTIVE RÉSUMÉ

Now that you're a soon-to-be college freshman, you'll need to make yourself as attractive to the job market as possible, because everyone needs experiential learning to complement the fields they are studying in school, and everyone needs to see what it's like in the workforce, if only to learn what you *don't* want to pursue. Getting a job requires that you have a clean, professional-looking résumé, and creating one isn't as difficult as you may think.

First things first: List all of your skills, honors, and accomplishments under proper bold headings.

What's your leadership experience? Did you lead a conference, project, series, club, or small business (or help a friend lead a business) during high school?

Are you a divergent thinker? Can you see things from many angles? A bipartisan type who has the talent of getting people to work together from across the aisles?

Be careful not to use trite buzzwords like "innovative," "cutting edge," "results-oriented," "dynamic," "self-motivated," "people-person," or "team player" to describe yourself. Recruiters read these and begin playing "baskets for dollars."

Revise and tailor your résumé slightly for every job application. The Lifehacker website suggests you rename your résumé each time you send it by adding the company name after yours: [firstname lastname] résumé for XXX company.doc. When the recruiter gets the attachment, he or she immediately knows that this résumé isn't just up to date but that it's built with this job in mind.

Employers and recruiters love to see community or public service; it shows that you're ready to put yourself on the line for others, that you have good time management skills (since presumably you've also been at school during your service experience), and that you have team skills (without having to say the overused buzz phrase "team player"). What did you accomplish through your community service? Add it to your résumé.

Your references must highly praise you—be sure you're giving the right ones. People who are not great at expressing superlatives should not be on your reference sheet. Also, be sure you stay in touch with your references so that a call from a prospective employer doesn't hit them the wrong way. No one likes to be used. Who should you ask for references? Teachers—preferably the same ones who referred you to college, your employer during high school, the CEO or director of whatever business or organization you may have volunteered for during high school, or your guidance counselor (but don't ask them from September through December, during peak college application hysteria).

If notification of your GPA or a list of specific courses studied are required by the company from which you seek employment, the recruiter will tell you. Recruiters often want to see things like SAT/ACT scores and GPA.

The important thing to remember about an initial internship résumé is that it's not only demonstrating the skills you presently have but the potential you have to learn new ones quickly on the job.

CHAPTER FOURTEEN

TOOLS THAT CAN MAKE THE DIFFERENCE

Until recently, there have been no great advances in the way high school students prepare for college. Just about everybody does the same thing in the same way: students go to see their school guidance counselor, consult big college directories, sit in review classes, study for various standardized tests, and maybe work one-one-one with a private college advisor if they can afford it. Aside from filling out forms online rather than on paper and receiving decisions through portals that have traffic jams at 6 p.m. on "decision day," not much is different in the application process from the time (long ago!) when I applied to college.

Well, that's what College Admission Central set out to change—in a really big way. We've developed new tools, apps, and information delivery systems to enable students to affordably get the help and guidance they need on demand, whenever and wherever they need it. Every student has the right to learn how to put his or her best foot forward in the admissions process!

ADMISSIONMAP

The first tool I'm going to highlight for you is called Admission-Map™. AdmissionMap is a "GPS for college application" that will navigate your path from high school to college. It contains nine multimedia modules to guide you along that stressful but exciting adventure:

1. Your Calendar: From High School to Acceptance

2. Things Admissions Won't Tell You

3. College Admission Action Plan

4. Choosing Your College

5. Template Letters

6. Big Data and the New Admissions Game

7. Mastering the Interview

8. Selecting the Best Safety Schools

9. Résumé and Senior Summer Skills

AdmissionMap is like having a highly experienced, caring college coach at your side, giving you the insider tips and essential strategies you need to win at the admissions game. College Admission Central's exclusive technology delivers this information to you, exactly when you need it most. View the modules on your phone, tablet, computer, or any Internet-connected device, and download the notes, supplements, and audio podcasts for offline review. Each module is logically divided into chapters and slides, giving you random access to any element through the intelligent interface. There's nothing else like it available anywhere.

ESSAYSUITE

Many students feel that *the* most challenging aspect of applying to college is writing a standout personal statement and preparing all the supplemental application essays for each school. To begin with, essay writing doesn't come naturally to everyone. To make matters worse, there are special "rules" that apply to application essays. That's why, each year, parents pay thousands of dollars to essay coaches and editors to help their kids develop winning essays.

At College Admission Central, we wanted to provide a more economical alternative for our clients. That's what led to the development of our groundbreaking technology product EssaySuite™. As its name implies, EssaySuite is a collection of tools and resources to help you brainstorm, draft, and polish a powerfully unique personal statement and prepare your supplements. There are four main components:

(1) Essay How-To Guide. A comprehensive multimedia resource with modules covering the essential aspects of essay prep:

- Brainstorming Your Essay
- Starting and Ending Your Essay
- Choosing Your Essay Topic
- Perfecting Your Essay

- Application Essay Examples

- Short Answer Questions

- The Why Essay

(2) Grammar Tips. A concise reference of the special grammar rules that apply to college application essay writing.

(3) Essay Critiques. Winning essays deconstructed by an admissions expert and an AP English teacher, showing you exactly how and why these essays helped secure admission to some of the most selective colleges.

DO YOU FIT INTO THE BOXES ON THE COMMON APPLICATION?

It's a serious question, so I'll ask it again: Can you describe yourself and your achievements in words and numbers alone? Many students cannot. Especially those with a visual story to tell Admissions, like debaters, athletes, performing artists, scientists who present at science fairs, student government leaders, hands-on service providers/young social entrepreneurs, and public speakers.

At College Admission Central, we've developed a unique, responsive web app and presentation platform to convey your personal story and accomplishments. It's called ResuMotiv™, and it creates an extraordinary multimedia résumé—a beautiful, professional format (including music) that will impress admissions officers and scholarship committees—and make you stand out. By the time admissions officers see your high school talents and accomplishments on the screen, they feel like they've met you, are impressed by you, and will more likely move you on to final committee. Think of your college presentation this way: when you have to give your dog a pill, you *could* wrestle him to the ground, pry open his jaws, shove the pill down his throat, and hold the jaws closed until he swallows it. *Or* you could slip the pill into an appetizing morsel of meat that he'll happily gulp down and know that he will receive the benefits without trauma. I'm here to tell you that getting your talents and accomplishments noticed by Admissions is not a very different process!

We must use new methods that are creative and eye-catching to showcase students' talents and experiences and mix them in with the traditional standards of transcript, scores, recommendations, and essays. You see, we slip the new in with the old to ensure that the admissions officer notices you and your uncommon flags. This gives you an advantage over other applicants.

ResuMotiv takes all your media (videos, audios, photos, PDFs, slides, and links) and creates a totally professional custom presentation in a format welcomed by decision makers. You can create and display your ResuMotiv presentation on any Internet-connected device. We include high quality hosting with a personalized (private) link that you can share with whomever you choose. No YouTube worries about inappropriate content or advertisements ruining your presentation.

If you wish, you can create multiple ResuMotivs, each for a different purpose—scholarship, college, conservatory, competitions, competitive boarding school applications during high school, and so on—even customize them to target the individual colleges to which you're applying. You can learn more by visiting www.ResuMotiv.com.

ACCEPTANCEMENTOR

As great as technology is, there is still no substitute for one-on-one time with a subject matter expert. That's where AcceptanceMentor™ comes in. It's our unique service offering where you can book time with our college advisors, myself, or with our INTEL-ISEF affiliated Director of Science Research (if you are interested in finding a lab research position/program or are working toward writing and submitting a science research paper to a regional, national, or international science fair). There's even an exclusive hotline service you can access whenever you need quick answers to tough questions or require some on-demand coaching and advising.

I invite you to explore all the ways College Admission Central can give you an advantage when applying to college and ultimately help you get accepted to your top choice and best fit schools. Please visit www.CollegeAdmissionCentral.com and our Facebook page for tons of free resources and invaluable tips.

IN CLOSING...

TO YOU, MY STUDENT DREAMER, ON YOUR EXTRAORDINARY ADVENTURE

Imagine being able to find out what you're made of, to begin a thrilling and totally new journey unlike anything you have ever done before: writing a book, starting a little business, advocating for a cause by public speaking, learning new foreign languages, doing bench research that could change the course of a disease, getting an idea for an app and finding the resources to build it, taking your talents to conservatory or art school and training to see how far you can go, making a film about a subject close to your heart, studying courses on a college campus that you've only dreamed about, founding an organization that will help the world or your community in a novel way—and doing it before you've even gotten to college. Imagine working and building and succeeding, or failing and then succeeding, or just failing, but joyously, because you've at least tried. What a fascinating narrative you would create for yourself! How much better you would know yourself! What belief you would have in yourself—finally knowing that you tried something extraordinary with your own hands, following your own passions! It will be the beginning of finding the "why" in your life...and on the way to finding yourself in life you will have discovered a bit more about your "why" for college.

So, young dreamer, you must stop thinking of high school as a pit stop on the way to *real school*. High School is a vibrant, "open all night" laboratory in which to begin creating yourself. And college is not a terminus where you graduate and step off the life platform— it's just another vehicle through which to continue building your personal narrative with the strengths and talents you've already discovered on your way to that place. How much fuller will your college career be after taking some unusual steps in high school and living out of the box and out of the walls of that building? How much more interesting will you be as a person? How much more empowered will you feel when you're ready to make the decision; "What will be my academic, social, and *dream* laboratory for the next four years?"

Take the time now, in high school, to be the strongest academician you can be and the most fertile spinner of dreams. Then, leave school behind at the bell, and start the adventure of finding your authentic self...not just for college, but for life. You won't believe what you can do!

"You have brains in your head. You have feet in your shoes.
You can steer yourself any direction you choose.
You're on your own. And you know what you know.
And YOU are the one who'll decide where to go..."
– Dr. Seuss, *Oh, The Places You'll Go!*

BONUS: College Strategy Video Session

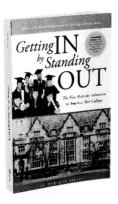

CPSIA information can be obtained at www.ICGtesting.com
Printed in the USA
BVOW02s1559250516

449539BV00036B/588/P